The Power of OUTRAGEOUS Expression

Hélène Musso

DEDICATION

I dedicate this Outrageous book to all of those who have supported me, believed in me and listened to my ramblings about having a voice and who have given me the opportunity and the confidence to express myself for the benefit of others. I can only hope that this book and my work in general will inspire you to express yourself and give you the courage to speak up!

THE 5 KEYS TO UNLOCK YOUR OUTRAGEOUS EXPRESSION

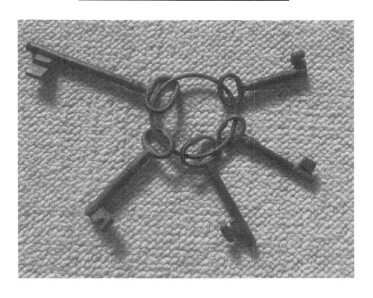

1. *Be Yourself*
2. *Be Kind to Yourself*
3. *Practise*
4. *Have Fun*
5. *Discover your Extraordinary Story*

CONTENTS

FROM THE HEART

"Hélène came to stay with me in the summer, after almost a year of working with her online and communicating on SKYPE, this huge French bundle of energy was coming to stay with me and my twins, and bringing her son too. I was very nervous, conversations were very fast online and I felt a bit overwhelmed at having all that energy with me in person. But when I met her she was calm and smiling, and much smaller than I'd imagined her. After a day or so into the visit I told her how I'd felt about her coming, she just smiled and told me she always came with the attitude that everything would be ok and it generally was.

That pretty much sums up Hélène's approach to life and her work. She left me with a mind-map of words to do some work with and they were all positive. Towards the end of 2014 I was working part-time as a freelance transcriber and proof reader and looking to expand my client list. Hélène contacted me on skills website asking general questions about transcription equipment, through that initial contact I began learning how to be a

1

Virtual Assistant, a job description I had never heard of before.

Working with Hélène has not only broadened my own skill-set in the world of social media, websites and digital editing, it has also brought me into contact with her inspirational way of being. A world where the strains of daily life are not problems but an opportunity to examine and prioritise what is important. To focus on now rather than worrying about the next thing and seeing new challenges as a chance to grow into the person we want to become." **Liz Ware**

....

"I have seen Hélène for some months now for her coaching services and can highly recommend them. She is very talented, a great listener and really knows how to get the best out of people.

My story: I have so many niggling issues, complaints, gripes, frustrations and seditious views about life, relationships, work, morals, ethics and really anything to do with 'other people' that I couldn't wait, in my characteristic doom and gloom style, to start chipping away at and eroding

Hélène's resolve, ebullient personality and general happiness in all things.

After the first few sessions it became very clear that Hélène was the one doing the chipping and eroding and not the other way round! After several sessions (and much resistance on my part) we had proved that many of my issues have no grounding whatsoever and no matter how it seemed to me back then I don't have any 'proof' that everyone and everything is against me! I don't 'know' what people are thinking about me and the situations I am in. Wow, I didn't see that coming!!!

Hélène and I, now we have identified certain weaknesses in my outlook to almost any given situation, are now working on techniques and strategies to diffuse the negative thoughts before they become a problem for me and others. I really like the role plays and the role reversal techniques Hélène employs in her sessions and it gives me a chance to practise these new skills.

For me (and I am sure the approach will change for each individual's needs) the sessions are free-flowing and spontaneous and this stops them becoming dull and monotonous. I enjoy this and

3

Hélène uses her knowledge of drama improvisation to good effect here making it fun as well as informative.

In a 'testimonial' I guess you would expect me to say that 'life has never been better, I am so happy, I love life and I love being alive' blah blah blah. I am not sure I can say THAT but I honestly do feel more in control of myself, my thought processes, the difficult situations I find myself in and I am certainly more positive in my outlook to life. Hélène and I have a long way to go but I can start to look to the future with brighter anticipation and a lot more focus!

Hélène has really helped me (where many others have tried and failed) and for this I thank her!"

(This Client has asked me not to reveal their name)

....

"Thank you so much. I just have the unfaltering belief that everyone has the right, the duty and the responsibility to have a voice."
Hélène
Summer 2015

THE 5 KEYS TO UNLOCK YOUR OUTRAGEOUS EXPRESSION

Introduction

INTRODUCTION

Life is very simple, it is about motivation, mindset and practice, so...

1. Are you motivated enough to become outrageous?

If you are ready to hear the sound of your own outrageous voice and to be proud of it, even if you do not know *where* to start and just the idea makes you feel weak at the knees, then carry on reading this book!

"Insanity is doing the same thing over and over again, but expecting different results."

This quote is attributed to Albert Einstein but nobody really knows who said it. Maybe it doesn't matter *who* said it. Maybe all you need to ask yourself right now is: "Am I acting insanely?" If you eat chips every day of your life and you have your arteries blocked by the time you reach 40, you know why, right? This is the same thing. If you feel that what you have to offer is bigger than you and you cannot quite express it, then you have two choices.

Your low-impact choice is to read books to discover what the problem is, I did that for years because I just like learning. It never occurred to me that I really needed to *apply* some of their ideas! Do you know what? *that* way of thinking has held me back in other parts of my life, too. For example, it took me over two years to come to terms with the idea that Social Media might be an asset to my business. I just wanted to learn a bit about the internet but not enough to make a difference. It is when I decided to *apply* that knowledge and those skills that I started to make a difference to my life.

Or, you feel the anxiety rising, (yes, I can feel it with you, I still feel the void from time to time when something is new!) and y**ou engage with your desire to change and apply what you learn.**

1st word of caution though: This book is not a quick fix for your problems. I am not a fairy and I do not wave a magic wand! I wish! It will help you to change *only* if you want to! It is not going to give you a magic pill but it will be **magical** if you *apply* some of the ideas and techniques.

2nd word of caution: Time

First NEVER EVER tell me you have not got any time. We all have 24 hours a day, we are all given the same time, and time does not change, but how we use our time determines what comes next. Saying "I never have enough time", or "I do not have time" is often an excuse for not facing the real issues. **We always make time for what is important to us**. If you think that your happiness and expression are important, then you will make time to explore some of these ideas in my book. This change process will take time and the more time you take, the more likely you are to change. Have the courage to start, now!

Allow events to happen and value and relish the distractions - the kids, the dogs, the cats, the house, the spouse - because when you are on a journey of change, if you obsess about it, you will make yourself very ill. Treat time as your **ally** and travel with me on the wind or breeze of change. Please, please, enjoy it even if it is SCARY. If you like you are on a roller-coaster, then you are in for a treat. Feel the exhilaration of going up and down! The anxiety will evaporate as your confidence and your happiness grow.

3rd word of caution: There is **NO RIGHT OR WRONG** in all this process; this is about **YOU.** You are unique and we are going to experiment together over the course of this book. Never think that because one person says it, it's right. *Right* is what *feels right for you* and as long as you do not kill the old lady across the road - just joking - then you can do exactly what you think is *right* for you. Enjoy the ride!

4th: **Enough!** Let's get on with becoming outrageous! Let's take some risks on the roller-coaster of life!

2. How to use this book.

This book is full of stories.

Each story has a reason, a moral, an imperative need to express a basic truth.

Some stories are funny, some are mundane, some are just plain.

They are true stories; they have not been invented but they invite you to reflect on your OWN story, to discover your own EXTRAORDINARY story.

The book also is also full of games and exercises.

These work best if you engage with them - so don't just read through them, do them! After all, practice makes perfect!

If you want to carry on exploring, why not try one of my courses?

They will put what you learn here in context and will give you an opportunity to practise.

For more details, have a look at my website:

http://www.Hélènemusso.co.uk

ARE YOU READY FOR AN OUTRAGEOUS LIFE?

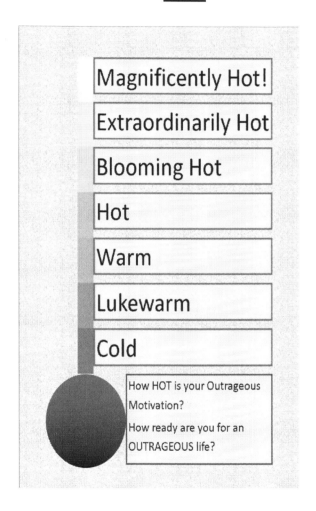

About selfishness: this book is not about promoting your ego and your selfishness by being more outrageous.

It **is not** about being arrogant and thinking that you deserve everything. It is about finding yourself but with integrity and with respect for others and with humility.

Whatever your past has been, you can change for the better and instead of becoming a victim of your circumstances, reclaim your life so that you can be happy but also kind to others.

Are you ready for an <u>Outrageous</u> Life?

How hot is your Outrageous Motivation today?
Cold, Lukewarm, Warm, Hot, Blooming Hot,
Extraordinarily Hot or Magnificently Hot?
Put a large circle in your favourite colour around the
one(s) which tempt you!

Who is an outrageous role-model for you?
Who else would you like to be and why ?
What are the qualities that attract you to that person?
Write down 3 qualities of that outrageously
expressive individual that *you* specifically want to
acquire.

Be **excited by change!** What if you were to be excited
instead of being scared?
Have you had an exciting holiday recently or can you
picture the best holiday you ever had?

Living the Outrageous Life is like riding on the
rollercoaster of life and loving every minute of it.
(I may not be a fan of real-life roller-coasters but love
my life for its excitement and joie de vivre!)

3. Outrageous: An attempt at a definition.

Outrageous is such an interesting word as it can be both negative and positive. It has an appeal but also can evoke very negative emotions. By choosing such an extreme word, I invite you to consider what it means to you.

Is it stepping out of your comfort-zone and claiming your place in the world? Is it acknowledging your own grandeur and beauty? When you feel small inside, ask yourself *"who wants to be let out to play?"* Is it you? **Peek a boo, it *is* YOU**! Being outrageous does not mean you dress or behave in a rude or inappropriate manner but just that you allow yourself to really thrive and make a mark on the world around you, by **being YOU totally, unashamedly, proudly.**

Take the **polarity game** and list the positive and negative connotations of such an outrageous word. If you like that word, what does it create in you? But also, in which way might it repulse and frighten you?

THE POLARITY GAME

The Polarity Game

In a battery, we have two polarities, labelled on either end of the battery as - and + .

Without the polarities, the battery would not work. Negative does not necessarily mean something bad but something that needs to be recognised, accepted and released. Then, you need to ask yourself what do I want instead?

Consider the word OUTRAGEOUS.

What are the positive and negative polarities of the word, for you?

Negative Outrageous	Positive Outrageous
e.g rude, over-the-top	e.g. brilliant,

Be warned: If you become outrageous, you might lose some friends as some may not like the change in you. If they are fools, they will not support you, but if they can see the beauty and the flower blossoming in you then, these people are your real friends and the others will disappear into oblivion. **By the way this book is not for women only. Men equally need to find their beauty within.**

I like the following words (if they help):

"Flamboyant, flashy, dazzling, saucy, shameless, brazen, brash, unspeakable, adventurous, bold, daring, audacious". Get yourself a **thesaurus** and find the one that resonates with you and with **you** only!

MY OUTRAGEOUS CHANGE STORY

I started my outrageous "change" story with a group called Damsels In Success. I had heard they helped women in business and out of the blue, out of intuition, I booked myself into their main conference in November 2011.

There were about 100 of us, all women. And we stood at the beginning and were asked to sing along to the song "Fireworks" by Katie Perry. I had heard the song but never paid attention to the content and spurred on by the atmosphere of the group, I got up, started singing and then became completely overwhelmed and burst into tears.

This precise moment was when I understood I needed to change! I needed to shape my life instead of just accepting it! I needed to take charge and lead my life instead of just being led by it! It took a few years to reflect and decide what I was going to do... but.

I enrolled on John Seymour's NLP (Neuro Linguistic Programming) coaching course and qualified in 2014 as a coach. I set up Public Speaking Demystified later in 2014 and the rest is history, as they say...

THE 5 KEYS TO UNLOCK YOUR
OUTRAGEOUS EXPRESSION

Part 1: Are You
Being Yourself?

ARE YOU BEING YOURSELF?

I want to talk about something that might sound very strange because it should be obvious. It's being yourself. I will use a quote, allegedly, from Oscar Wilde:

> *"Be yourself, everybody else is taken."*

I love the tongue in cheek quality of this rather outrageous statement but it summarises my outlook on life.

What do you mean, **being yourself**? We are what we are! Can we be anything else? To the outside eye, yes, we are. We have a name, a place of origin, of living, a car, or not, some possessions or not a lot. We are born, we live and we die. That is very simple and it is the cycle of life. From the time of our birth, we are conditioned by two things, genes and society (including family). Somehow we cannot do anything about either. Being yourself is about not being dependant and stuck with our genes and society but embracing fully both of these entities, on our own terms.

When I start talking about being yourself, I am asking you, then, to make abstraction of genes or society and to fully embrace who **YOU** are in the deep core of your individuality. YOU can only be yourself if you feel a deep sense of identity and fulfilment at the core of your being. I believe that a lot of us only scratch the surface in terms of that fulfilment and live lives which are only half lived. It does not have to be that way. YOU and YOU alone can start a journey to find yourself and I hope this book will make a contribution towards that aim.

In order to do that, YOUR first step is to acknowledge **your own uniqueness.** You are the only person like YOU on the planet. You are different from anyone else, even if you are an identical twin got a twin, you are two different individuals, with your funny face, your quirkiness, your accent, your background, your hand gestures, your pompous phrases and your silly smile.

On a trip, years ago with my first partner, I was rather depressed and I remember comparing myself to an ant in an ant colony and actually seeing myself as a person whose existence was small and not important. I could be easily be replaced by another hard-working ant, stuck in a repeated pattern of behaviour. My partner had a much more positive view of himself. He saw himself as a strong bull ready for anything!

It is therefore extremely important to acknowledge **who you are**. If you have a soft voice, you will bring a softness and gentleness to your expression. If you are quite scatty, that is how you are going to interact with people. There is nothing wrong with the way you are. Tall, short, big or thin, black, white, yellow, colours of the rainbow - sorry just joking - you ARE just fine. You are just YOU.

Better you are special and unique. One and only.

1. About Your Name.

Being yourself is, first of all, about your identity. It starts as simply as your **name** - Your name, who you are with that name and where you come from.

I used to call myself *"Helen"* in my first six months of living in England. But my name is not *"Helen"*, it looks like *"Helen"*, but it's *"Hélène"* (You pronounce it Elaine really but it is still not quite exact. Or maybe, for the Anglo-Saxons, I should spell it LN, which would be close enough!). After six months of not replying when a friend called me - not a good one if you are in the pub waiting for a drink - as it felt alien to hear these sounds, I just thought *"It's not me!"* It wasn't right, it didn't feel right. I could not respond to *"Helen"*.

In my desire to be integrated, I was denying my own core identity, starting with the way I had been named as a child. I had to accept that, despite all my best intentions, I would never be English and did it matter anyhow? I realised later on, that my Frenchness in England was my best asset as I was different from everyone else and got noticed for being different. Especially if I could get away for not queuing like everyone else and bringing blue cheese to my childminder for my daughter's packed lunch!

Recently my son was at the swimming pool, and he met a little friend in his diving class called Pip. And I straight away said *"Pip! That's a strange name"* So I asked my son to check if his real name was not Philip or something, but it was not, it was Pip. Then I reflected: *"So he must be called Pip, that's what he's called. Although for me it's a bit of a strange name but that's the way he is. It is him, let's call him Pip."*

I think your name is paramount in defining YOU and it is essential to **value your name** for shaping and making YOU the way you are. With the foreign nationals I work with, it is even more important to ask them what they *want* to be called, not what they think is acceptable in an English speaking country.

I recently worked with a South American lady called Maria. In my workshops I always make sure we learn all the participants' names and call them exactly as they would like to be called, out of respect for their identity. When asked what she would like to be called, she actually gave us the whole of her name Maria-Carmen and she realised she wanted to use her full name as it was an integral part of her identity as a foreigner and so that is what we called her in the workshop. I don't think she had ever been asked: what do you *really* want to be called?

Again, when someone uses a shorter version of their name, for example a Matthew might become a Matt, I always double check what they ultimately prefer to be called. When you call an individual exactly by the name they cherish or at least they are used to, then you increase your connection with that person and very simply build a rapport whilst showing respect for them as individual.

Now it is your turn!

Try the **You Are Your name Show** game

Have fun!

Welcome to the
You Are Your Name show!

Enjoy!

Recently, in one of my workshops I had two participants who did not like their names. My immediate response was to feel saddened.

Then I suggested, "Is there any chance you can change your name? If not, what about creating a story about yourself which would make you proud? What about inventing a story about something you wish had happened to you?"

There was a bit of confusion from the bemused participants whose immediate response was that this would be a lie.

"A lie?" I replied, "Are you sure? If it is a story that makes you happy and proud and enables you to live a more positive life then is it not worth thinking about?

THE CROCODILE STORY

I have a scar on my right knee. It's the result of a moped accident at 15, but I decided that it would be fun to pretend that I had been bitten by a crocodile during one of my travels. Much more exotic and fun - and just about possible!

So when my son has a little friend round to our house, we talk about the scar and the crocodile.

My son, although he knows the true story, tells the crocodile story with great relish to his friends and is now an expert at filling in the details so that it sounds true to all around him.

Are we telling a lie?
No - we are creating a memory which makes us laugh and could - potentially - have happened!

*Would it be fun to create a
crocodile story of your own?*

So - now it's your turn!

What is the story of your name?
Why were you given that name?,
What is the origin of your name?
Most importantly what does this
name mean to you?
Do you need to invent your own
"Crocodile Story"?

You will find lots of information on
the internet about the origins of
your name and some interpreta-
tions of your personality directly
linked to your name.

Take what is useful and relevant to
you and discard the rest.
YOU have to decide.

SIMPLE-NOT OUTRAGEOUS, SORRY! TIPS ON REMEMBERING NAMES

Arggh, I can never remember anyone's name!

Why is remembering names good for you?

- Mutual respect
- Feel good factor
- Increase connection
- Validate others
- Develop mutual understanding
- Increase cooperation
- And on a selfish note, you never ever know when you may need that person, one day, the plumber, the friend who said....

SO,

☐ Make remembering names a priority! On a scale of 1 to 10, how important is it to you? (10 being very important). If it is not that important, then your brain will not store that information, so if it has to be important, make it important if you would like it to be! *We remember in life what really matters to us.* If not remembering your wife's birthday means that she is likely to sulk for weeks, maybe it is time to learn the date of her birthday. I am not very good with birthdays as for me, they are just other dates in the calendar but I always send flowers to my mother on her birthday and never forget the date. Why? I know it makes her happy. My dad, on the other hand, acts similarly to me and is rather detached from birthday celebrations and would not be offended if I forgot. I have on numerous occasions forgotten his birthday!

☐ Repeat the name several times so that it sticks in your head. I often say, "Pip, is it? that's an interesting name" or "Fiona, that's a lovely name", or ask them to repeat so that I can hear their name and they also feel connected.

☐ Repeat that new name in your head before you go and do something else.

☐ If the name is difficult for you, ask them to spell it and even write it down as soon as you can.

☐ Let go of worry, if you forget: ask again but with a big smile, *"I am so sorry but I did not catch your name"* or *"I have forgotten your name and I really feel a bit silly! I have been talking to you for a while and have realised that I do not know your name!"* People like when you acknowledge your own imperfections and have the courage to ask. Often they do not know your name either!

☐ You are not alone in struggling to remember-we are more likely to remember someone who had an impact on us, small or big. Associate the name with a location, the one where you met that person or an item that that person might be wearing.

In my workshops, I play name games and this is my favourite one.

☐ All participants stand in a circle
☐ I make sure everyone has heard everyone's name by going round the circle
☐ Adam starts by making eye contact with another participant, Beth for example, and then says her name
☐ Adam starts walking towards Beth
☐ Beth look at Callum across the circle and says his name
☐ Beth starts walking towards Callum

- [ ] By that time, Adam has reached Beth's position and stands in her place
- [ ] Callum chooses Debbie and then the game carries on and on.

This game has a layered effect and it is not a cake!
Shame, is it not time for lunch!

1. It allows everyone to get connected through hearing each other's names

2. It is an ice-breaker

3. It reinforces concentration

4. It often creates laughter

5. It creates rapport and communication

6. It encourages eye contact and develops confidence

It is definitely the best game to allow you to remember names!!

Look at this beautiful wall with the stones neatly stacked up. The 'layered effect' is like building a wall and laying one set of stones at the time, layer by layer. I believe that it is the best to we learn. Layer by layer from the bottom up and then we can contemplate the "construction" we have made in our lives.

2. About Your Mannerisms.

Your **mannerisms** make you unique, fun and funny and most importantly make you human. Relish them! If you have seen one of my videos or seen me in the flesh, you will know that I speak quite fast, obviously with a soft French accent. I have a tendency to move my head and to look to the side while I collect my thoughts.

I will use my hands to describe what's happening. Maybe it is because I am from the South of France, or because I am possibly part Italian, or because I'm quite dramatic in the way I am, but it's just me. Originally, I was a little bit scared to be me, but I started teaching Drama so I suppose that between my natural tendency to be overdramatic and my chosen profession, I just had to accept it. Large gestures are just there and it is part of me, I can't fake it. So, if you're NOT like me, that's fantastic; I'm not sure there's room for more! but there's nothing wrong with having mannerisms which are just part of you. They make **you who you are.**

I really like people who move slowly and speak slowly, as in contrast with my speed and dynamism. Do let other people see the beauty in your mannerisms. This applies to the way we speak too. Sometimes we feel *"Oh! I shouldn't say that."* Or *"I should say it like that."* Or *"There's something wrong with me, because I speak too fast or I speak too slowly".*

Let me repeat it: there is nothing wrong with the way you are. You have to be in tune with this and be able to accept that you are the way you are. Being yourself means that you are able to tap into your own energy and radiate this energy towards others. Unlike your name, your mannerisms are part of your cultural and genetic inheritance and you cannot change them so **learn to love them.**

What is the point otherwise? A life of angst and regret. Just imagine that if we were all Dolly the sheep clones, life would be a little bland and boring so embrace your quirkiness, your differences, your whole self!

To get you into a feeling of greater comfort with your mannerisms, have a go at the Spy Game.

PLAY THE SPY GAME

Spend the day observing people's mannerisms-the way they move, the way they talk, the way they hold their body, the sounds they utter, how they use their hands. What do you notice about them?

Then **listen, hear, watch, smile and have fun**! This is a game I used to teach as part of my drama classes and it brought a lot of spontaneous laughs as the students came back from an hour observing passers-by at the town centre.

It has the added advantage of making trainee performers very aware of how they use their bodies for different types of roles. In your case, I am asking you to notice and enjoy the way you move!

Be a Spy for a day

Spend the day observing people's mannerisms. Notice the way they move, the way they talk, the way they hold their body.

What do you notice about them?

Pay attention to the sounds they utter, and how they use their hands. Then listen, hear, watch, smile and have fun!

Spy on yourself

Spend a day or a couple of hours or just
start with a few minutes here and there.

Ask your good friends
"What mannerisms do you like in me?"
What do I do which makes me unique
and different?"
Listen to what they say, and appreciate
their feedback!

My daughter Lily makes silly little sounds
when she is startled and when she inter-
acts with others. Her friend Ellen loves it
because it makes her sound different
and spontaneous and very young. It is
appealing and funny and cute.
We are laughing at her but more laughing with her!

Spy on Yourself - continued

Have you ever heard the comedian Jimmy Carr?
He has the most irritating laugh but he acknowledges it as part of his act. On the Internet, it is even called his "signature laugh."

Jimmy has made a deliberate and conscious decision to use it. It's a bit like Marmite - you either love it or hate it - but it does seem to draw a fair few fans towards him.

Observe yourself when **you** interact. This is more difficult than watching other people, but if you pay attention, you will be able to hear your own laugh, the expressions you use a lot, and the overall way in which you deal with the people, situations and events around you.

Play Spy kids with your kids

Send your children to observe how passersby walk and then ask them to copy it and exaggerate the walk.

Do this in private, if you want to be outrageous - you still have to consider other people's feelings - but it will create a lot of fun and lots of laughter.

Have you enjoyed the Spy game or have you been too shy to do it? Drop me a line on Social media. I look forward to seeing you on my courses, of course!

WHAT PEOPLE HAVE SAID ABOUT HÉLÈNE'S COURSES

"Hélène created a safe, nurturing environment where we started the process of communicating and expressing ourselves with vulnerability and with confidence"

Julia Meehan-Thompson

....

Whatever you discover with these exercises, let it happen!

NO JUDGMENT ALLOWED!
NO:-
"I should be like that!"
"Oh, gosh, is it really me?"
"I should be like her or him!"

41

You are just fine, just the way you are!

Not everyone is going to like you but really, do you want to be liked by the riff raff down the road or do you want to be liked by the people who are close to you and understand you? If you feel nobody does, then ask yourself: is that true and what am I going to do about it? Is it time for change?

The choice is yours!

CULTIVATE YOUR SIGNATURE TALK, LAUGH, GESTURE, EXPRESSION:

It is so endearing when you are *yourself*. I have realised that I use the phrase "a fair amount" a lot when describing a lot of something and it is comical and rather ironic.

Years ago when working in a college, one student said to me, *"Every time you start a lesson Hélène, you always stand tall, scratch the back of your head, ruffle your hair, then clap your hands once and say loudly: "Right".* She added *"And we love it because it is YOU!"*

BE DARING, BE BRAVE, BE OUTRAGEOUS!

Video, moi, never!? Video yourself or ask your friends, spouse, kids to video you. Take part in presenting yourself to the world.

I ask participants to video themselves for a maximum of 1 minute and uncover their **"Extrrraordinary Storry."**

I would like to finish our chapter on Being Yourself with a teensy weensy simple, effective and reflective exercise aimed at wannabee speakers, which essentially makes you conscious of your own grandeur.

THE CIRCLE OF ASSURANCE

Being yourself means holding the space and having the courage to stand in that space.

I would like you to

- ☐ Stand up tall and close your eyes.
- ☐ Take 3 long deep breaths.
- ☐ Roll your shoulders back.

- Feel and think about being bigger, larger, taller, an invisible string is pulling your head gently towards the sky.
- Relax and move your arms around your body.
- Draw an imaginary circle in front of you, on the floor. It is your **Circle of Assurance.**
- Slowly step into that circle.

- When you are ready, visualise the type of audience you would like to be facing, a supportive audience.

45

- ☐ Open your eyes and look and "see" the audience.
- ☐ Feel the space.
- ☐ Stand tall, just be.

Enjoy that moment.

Stand still.

Hold it.

Enjoy.

3. About language: Play with language.

Tame your inner devil voice, bring out your angel voice!

Do you get so busy that your head starts to spin and you wish you could be somewhere else? I have moments like that when I just want to cultivate more stillness but can't seem to find the time to do it! Why, at times, is the brain playing tricks on us?

A STORY FROM THE PAST

I woke up two nights ago with a very silly problem which did not need much attention, but the little voice inside my brain was trying to convince me that it was an important matter.

I have an acquaintance who asked me if I could teach French to her son from September. When put on the spot, I did not react with enough finesse. The hourly rate I quoted seem too low to me and I forgot to mention terms and conditions, etc.

When I woke two nights ago, I could listen to this voice... "Why did you not ask for more?", "What if she is not happy with paying for a block of six lessons in advance?", "What shall I do about it now?" and so on.

The voice was getting louder to the point that I felt I needed to jump on the computer and send an instant message with all my demands and my terms and conditions.

But then I put on my sensible voice which said "just let go and get busy with something else". I did and I have not done anything about it and it is now not that important anymore.

I have now decided that if, by stating the price and the terms and conditions, I lose a potential client then this is a risk I take but is it that important? Is my life depending on it? Or is it just something that I have to go through? Whether it does materialise or not, it is not going to affect the rest of my life.

So next time the nasty evil voice takes over, just softly send the angel voice to the rescue!

The good news is that now re-reading that story two years later, I can tell you that my student prepared his GCSE and achieved an A*!

QUESTION TIME

Ask yourself the following question.

- In the grand scheme of things, is this problem that important or can I let it go?

- Sleeping on it - literally - might be the wisest decision you may make. If you sleep on it, won't it be squashed and then will diminish in size? Is it not the reason why we use that expression?

- If in doubt wait! The problem often sorts itself out and loses its importance.

MEET TWO PROTAGONISTS FROM YOUR LIFE

Who do you want to be your NUMBER 1?

FIND OUT WHO'S YOUR NUMBER 1!

MR NUMBER 1 DEVILISH VOICE	_MR NUMBER 1 ANGEL VOICE_
o Talks all the time with no breaths in between o Plays up the same scenario o Is cruel and nasty o Makes us feel small and stupid o Gets pleasure out of our pain o Makes us impatient	o Talks quietly in the background o Is too kind to always impose itself o Reassures us and makes us feel appreciated o Makes us appreciate others o Shows understanding and sympathy

and irritable
o   enjoys it when we
    pick on others

Mr Devilish Voice is the one protagonist who makes us scared.

It is the judging one, the one who feels that we are not good enough.

It's the one that says that the others are going to judge.

It's the one who is thinking too much that the audience is bored or disinterested when you make a presentation in public for example, the one who is loud and arrogant, the one you know you should never have accepted as a friend in the first place but seems to be often hanging around.

In other words, all these thoughts which make us

o   is persevering,
    patient and calm

Hearing the loud and brash voice of Mr Devilish Voice on a constant basis, Mr number 1 Angel Voice is more like the calm and assured Buddha we all wish we had in our hectic lives.

It does require perseverance and willingness to change that voice, to shift that demon voice to the angel voice with compassion and understanding.

Now this applies to men and women; men need that compassion as much as ladies but it is often seen as uncool or unmanly to show compassion and care for a man. One thing nobody really needs to worry so much the night before a presentation so that we do not sleep and end up being very tired the next day!

These feelings come from the demon voice inside us, the one who makes us doubt our abilities and who wants us to be perfect instead of just being ourselves.

It's the voice which says that nobody likes us and especially the one who says - *I do not like you very much* - to ourselves.

The one who constantly judges instead of supports, the one who is like the angry and demanding parent who makes our lives a misery or very uncomfortable.

The one who says *"Why do you even try, you will* know is that you are being compassionate to yourself.

They will see the results when you present yourself with determination and success.

Accepting yourself for who you are and being yourself is the key.

Be instead of doing, just be - aren't we human beings?

One of the reasons why we value the Demon within us is that we like the drama. The Angel often appears far too sensible and boring.

Once you realise that the drama is not needed to make you happy, then you listen to the Angel voice much more and you also start to listen to others *never succeed?"*

When we talk about presentations and public speaking, this nasty demon is in full flow and it is the reason why 1 in 4 people fear public speaking more than death.

attentively and compassionately.

By increasing your connection to yourself and to others, then you create a much more peaceful whilst fun and exciting reality.

ON SPEAKING IN PUBLIC

I think it's important to listen to these inner voices which let us down, so that we can shift and change the voice and rephrase it. Do not just deny the voice. Listen to it first and then change the words.

What about *"I am a person who has learnt a great deal over the years and has gained knowledge and skills, and I can therefore stand in front of you today"* or if you are younger and less experienced, what about *"I have researched my topic very well and I have acquired enough knowledge to get my point across, and for you to gain knowledge in return."* So, next time you have a doubt filling your head, catch yourself and rephrase the negative to a positive. It will take time to be established but it will bring peace of mind, I promise!

Play the Angel and Devil game

The Angel and Devil Game

In this game, you hear the devilish voice and you decide that you are going to use your angel voice, your kinder, more sympathetic voice. I have written an example for you. Keep the Angel as positive as you can. Listen to this inner voice, catch yourself and record what the devilish voice is saying to you.
Take your time to do this exercise. Have fun! if you get stuck, enrol a friend who is reading the book too and you can take it in turns to help each other! It is then much more powerful and empowering.

Devil	Angel
e.g. "I can't do this!"	"Yes, you can but you just need more practice, that's all"

Mini random outrageous filler

Is it Christmas already?!

LETTING GO EXERCISE

Fill the gap with your own words!

Ask yourself:

Is it that important that I do this......................?

(Write it down)

I worry about......................

Can I let ……………… go and let ……………..happen?

Is the world going to stop if I do not do

this…………………... or that…..……………..?

BEST TIP IF YOU PANIC!

Arrrggh!

 If the fear embraces you and your mind starts to race with negative thoughts, just pause, breathe deeply and listen and rephrase.

Have that dialogue every day, every time you feel overwhelmed by the demon voice.

Allow yourself time though: **Rome wasn't built in a day!**

Extra Extra Outrageous Tips
on speaking in public

Being scared is normal!
If you are never scared, somehow, it means you stopped caring.
The main thing to remember is to manage that fear so that you can function and deliver with presence and brio.
I am still very scared when I present and the first 10 minutes I always feel a bit wobbly.

However,
I have a strong belief that I can do it
I have a strong aim in mind.
I believe that my role is to inspire others to reach their potential
I am positive and passionate
I believe that people learn best by doing
I know about learning styles and how people learn at their best
I prepare and prepare to make sure my material is relevant and focused
I often have a plan B and C just in case which would be adaptations of Plan A and show flexibility of approach.
......and
Years of experience to support me if it does not go exactly according to plan!

I am experienced at facilitating a workshop and at making sure everyone is fully involved and engaged.

..and finally,
I care.

A STORY FROM THE PAST

In 2003 in the middle of my separation from my daughter's father, I made a promise to myself, the word "problem" will have to disappear from my vocabulary. It will be deleted, annihilated, conquered and tamed, like a victorious Roman centurion in his battle to conquer the world.

I felt like Julius Caesar at the height of his power! I very soon realised that not only I needed to rub out and make some words disappear but I also needed to start looking for replacements. The word **problem** *is now, in my mind, either*

-Things I have to do

-Challenges

-Opportunities

In the **things I have to do**, *I remember clearly, a few years back, finding it difficult to organise my children's lives and their activities especially for after school and holidays. I was making it a "problem". It was "problematic" to do all this. It was like a "chore", another word I do not use as it makes me shiver with distinct repulsion.*

Once I had understood that being a parent comes with some responsibilities, and was therefore part and parcel of being a parent, but not necessarily a "problem" but just "things I had to do in everyday life" suddenly it was much easier to organise their outings and social lives.

With "challenges" and "opportunities", I put the power back firmly in my camp instead of being the victim of a problem falling on me. It gave me more control and therefore made more sense in my life and I felt relieved and more enthusiastic. Stuff happens but when it is not seen as a problem, we just deal with it as best as we can without getting as emotionally engaged as before and in a more poised and calm manner.

Fabulastic Word Swap

Pick a word you dislike: homework, for example and see if you can find a replacement word; the choice is yours

Best outrageous tip : find a thesaurus and use the antonyms, you can even play it with your children!

Extraordinary extra tip: My son was asked to use a prefix to create a new word and invent a definition for it. He chose supergem: a gem which is able to re-produce other gems. Just think about it : this is another way of looking at wealth. If only gems were so easily available!

Use "fab" and "fantastic" in your everyday language and you are going to feel more fab and fantastic!
Have a fab day!

YOUR FABULASTIC WORD SWAPS

Old Word	New Word
e.g. homework	homeplay

SHOULD I STAY OR SHOULD I GO?

"Should-ism" is a disease which permeates the English language with judgment and scorn. So start noticing when you use "should". Is it when you blame yourself? Living with regrets is not helpful. We live in the present and can influence our future but the past has gone so why regret it? It is too late, anyhow. **Learn** from the past but let it go.

"I should have done that!" Or is it? *"I should do that"* after someone else has imposed an action/direction on you that you may not want to take?

Then mentally, erase it with your magic fun-looking eraser/rubber!

Then replace it by: *"I could have done that but I did this instead and that is fine. I have done it now and the past is gone, I can only live in the present and take the consequences if any".*

"Should" creates a culture of guilt whereas *"I could"* gives you the opportunity to reflect. *"I could do that"* but I might or might not do that. Equally watch for *"I have to"* and think instead of *"I have a choice"* in the matter.

So a good one is *"I choose to do that and take the consequences whatever they are".* This again puts the ball back in your camp and you are in control of the process and you will feel much lighter for it!

Best Outrageous Tip:

Ban "should" from your vocabulary!
Every time you use it , start again.
Play with words and congratulate yourself for banishing it!

OR
Write "should" on a piece of paper screw it up in a ball...and.. jump on it (ask the kids) Spit on it or let the kids do it- please in the garden- we might get some germs! Burn it ritualistically whilst singing "Banished! Banished! Banished!" as if you were an Indian chief. **Outrageous alternative:** throw it in the sea on the way to a nice holiday....OR.... cut each letter separately and burn them one by one. **Luxury Outrageous Tip:** Ask the kids to fine you every time you say "should" (they will become rich if you are currently addicted)
OR
Find your own ritual I do burn paper when I want to let go and actually it is effective for ME Do what works for YOU!

When we are scared especially when speaking in public then, sometimes words escapes us. Sometimes we do not know why but we get the butterflies, the dry mouth, the pounding heart, the wobbly knees, the shaky hands. Where does this all come from? Why is it that we cannot fully control it and that some of us feel so unwell to the point of not functioning?

We want to look like this:

but we feel like <u>this</u> inside...

THIS IS WHERE IT ALL COMES FROM:

You are in the jungle and you hear background noises. You stop still and your heart starts to pound. You turn round and in the undergrowth you see the shape of a large and fierce jaguar and before you have time to think any further you see the large creature jumping towards you with force and hear the roar. Now the best response would to run (flight) but some of us would freeze and the brave ones would fight (fight). Personally, I think I would run and scream!

The **fight-or-flight response** (also called the **fight-or-flight-or-freeze response**, **hyper-arousal**, or the **acute stress response**) is our response to stressful situations. It comes from the sympathetic nervous system which sends signals to our bodies, in the form of unpleasant physical feelings. In our minds, we forget that we are sensory animals and that it is these senses that trigger our emotions and our behaviours.

Obviously, the likelihood of being attacked by a jaguar in the middle of London (or Paris) is pretty remote unless a local zoo has left a cage open by accident.

No, this is not the right picture; I want a scary big cat , change it! You can't get the staff these days!

BETTER AND SCARIER!

Just a last word to reassure. The acute stress response is **NORMAL**. What is NOT normal is to get overwhelmed. You have the power to change that feeling and to manage that fear. Have you ever thought of **"being" the jaguar** instead of being the scared little cat? Become the **tamer of your own emotions!**

THE 5 KEYS TO UNLOCK YOUR OUTRAGEOUS EXPRESSION

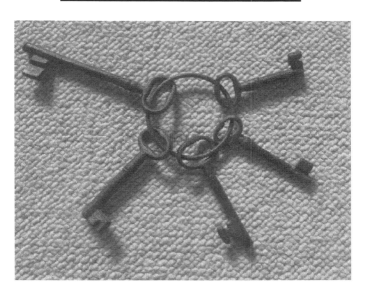

Part 2: Be Kind to Yourself

BE KIND TO YOURSELF

1. Get Your Mojo Back.

We are spending too much time denigrating ourselves, and being kind to ourselves is essential, so start with a little dose of Mojo. Before you think about changing the whole of yourself and having a personal revolution, what about reviewing what you have got **within** you, already?

I used to think that being kind was a weakness and that having compassion was being lazy. I even had contempt for the people who were a bit too *"nice"* as I equated *"being nice"* to *"being a bit of a door mat"*.

I remember the jokey but pertinent comment from one of my A level students when teaching Drama: *"Miss, you are like a little soldier"* as I was soldiering on, even with a large pregnant belly, determined to make sure that THEIR play was going to be the best ever.

Now I value kindness and I guard it but not like a soldier but more like a nurturing being who has come to realise that it is more than ok to be kind and by being kinder to others, I have started to be kinder to myself.

I still set high expectations of myself but I just acknowledge my imperfections. I take one step at a time and let go, most of the time, of guilt, and this makes me feel simply more content. Your best starting point and your best source of strength is to **re-engage with what has made you happy in the past.** It is also a good way to take stock and to re-evaluate your moves in life. You might have heard of the expression *"Get your Mojo back"* and it is used in some films. What I found fascinating is that such a simple expression has got some ingrained value in its cultural and social references to freedom, happiness and independence. Start now, be curious, and get your magic back!

Get your MOJO back!

Outrageous knowledge:

Mojo is a word from the black Creole culture of the coastal regions of South Carolina and Georgia and probably arrived in some form with the slaves from Africa.

The word means "magic," and although it has connections to drugs and sex, a Mojo is mainly a good luck charm enhanced through voodoo with the ability to cast a positive spell. Be aware, it is not about black magic but about positivity!
If you've got your Mojo working, then everything's going your way.

A Mojo is often made of red flannel cloth and tied with a drawstring, containing botanical, zoological, and mineral curios, petition papers, and is usually worn under clothing.

There are numerous videos online if you are creative enough to make a bag. If you do, take a photo, write a short description of the content of your bag and post it on my Facebook page either at Hélène Musso or Public Speaking Demystified-Tame the fear. You never know, there may be prizes for the best looking Mojo bag!

In the picture above, the little bags are full of lavender. I come from the south of France with a smell of lavender in the villages of Provence and fields bursting with purple flowers in the Summer. The little bags used to be put in the laundry cupboards to freshen sheets and, even if nobody ever said, they are there to make us smile and relaxed.

OUTRAGEOUS TONGUE-TWISTERS

I have to say a tongue twister!

The more your practise the easier it becomes!

Play them with your kids!

Try...
- o "Yellow lorry, red lorry,..."
- o "She sells sea shells by the sea shore."
- o A French one. Pourquoi pas?
  "Les chaussettes de l'Archiduchesse sont elles sèches, archi-sèches?"

When I started looking at names for my business, I chose the words **"Confidence Rejuvenation"**. Never ever ask a foreigner to pronounce the word rejuvenation, it is a real mouthful and I had to train myself to say it and with a copious amount of repetition and commitment, I eventually managed to say it!

One good tip if you are a foreigner, if you notice that one word you clumsily utter is definitely not understood by anyone, you have **two choices**:

- ☐ You either persevere or learn how to pronounce it and maybe take elocution lessons.

  ⬚ You chose a different word, a synonym
       which does not give you, or the people
       around you, a headache every time you use
       it!

This is not about being lazy but about being
practical! I am not looking for perfection here but
for communication and expression.

Let's make it simple.

With *"rejuvenation"*, all words started to come
flooding back, literally. The prefix RE comes from
Latin and means" again and again and again" using
the need for repetition but it also means going
back. **Bingo**, with such a word, I could look at the
future and practice for a better future whilst
completely embracing the past and learning from
the it. How fascinating! I am in love with RE , now it
is your turn!

The Outrageous Power of the Prefix RE
-Renew with life

-**Re-engage with yourself**: value the past build on it. If you have done it before, you can do it again
-**Renew with what you know**: find your stability in your own environment
-**Find your best ritual**: nurture it, polish it, use it, make everything settle around you
-**Re-invent your life**: with the old comes the new and you can do things you thought you may never do

Outrageous game: how many outrageous words can you find beginning with RE ?

e.g re-incarnated, re-juvenated, re......

2. Learn from your wobbles.

I am often told *"You look so confident"*, and overall I suppose I am. However, I was not always like that! On a regular basis, I have what I call *wobbles*, those little moments of crisis where the world comes crashing down and the only real desire is to find a mouse hole and to just disappear into it for a while.

I think these moments are normal. I used to fear them and to think I was inadequate. Now I embrace them and, more importantly, learn from them so that I can find a happy medium and more balance in my life. The wobbly bits make me laugh and, now I am getting older (only slightly though), I have started to get some more wobbly bits on my tummy! Does it not make me even more yummy!!? Sorry only being silly!

Earlier this year, I wrote a blog called *"Even confidence coaches have their wobbly moments"*. Enjoy the wobbly bits!

A STORY FROM THE PAST

Learning from your wobbles!

Yesterday, my morning started well and I trained a lovely group of ladies from Winning Women Essex in Public Speaking. I have had some focused and rewarding time for several weeks now and felt overall positive and elated.

Then by lunchtime, I was tired, rather grumpy and wanted to be left alone. I was having a wobble, a doubt crept into my head about the business, about the children, about living here about relationships... I started questioning myself. And, after a couple of hours feeling sorry for myself and having gobbled too many biscuits to keep my discomfort at bay, I thought, as a coach, what would be the best strategies I would advise my clients to keep themselves happier if not HAPPY, full stop?

Accept that there will be doubt at times and keep with that acceptance, stay with it, accept it but no judgment, it happens, we are human beings, not super-heroes!

Check if you are not tired: I decided to take time out that afternoon and slept for an hour and again fell asleep at 9.30 in front of the TV that evening - I was tired and needed to rest. Are you tired too? Most of us are exhausted by a long list of demands that we put on ourselves. It is sometimes needed but often self-inflicted. Slow down!

Step away: I ended up wanting to carry on working in my grumpy mood and decided to download photos from my beloved paradise Island La Reunion from a previous holiday. Everything from then went pear shaped with me deleting the photos from my phone before I had time to download them to my computer. I found them on Google photos but seemed to be unable to put them back on my computer creating a huge amount of frustration and pure, utter anger at myself for being so stupid.

Wrapped in my own indignation about my photos, I was ranting and then, my son - my children are much more sensible than me - sent me on my way to get myself busy with something else so that I could temporarily calm down. It was so much better afterwards. He wanted to play with the computer too so it was a good strategy for him to get me off it!

Ask for help: I asked three people to help me solve the photo issues and they all came up with good solutions which meant that I could retrieve my photos! I even got a lot of photos from a relative to replace the lost ones. When asking for help, I had to explain and own up, therefore display vulnerability and acknowledge my helplessness. But, by being honest, not one of them made me feel silly for having asked.

Be grateful.

I decided to finish my day being grateful for the people around me, my son and daughter, my friend Paul , my new lodger Neil, the group of ladies I train, Jane, Jackie, Rosemary, Julie, Sandra, the previous clients I have had like Beata and Bambi and Harriet. Many more I could thank too!

2. Acknowledge the little steps.

You might have noticed by now that I like sayings and quotes. I particularly like the following:

"Rome was not built in a day"

We want everything yesterday. We want money, we want to be successful, we want a big house. We want the most amazing relationship, we want everything and we want it now.

Unfortunately, we are not in dream land, we are in the real world. It doesn't mean it's always going to be difficult, but it's going to be a process, that there will be a sequence of events to take you from one place to another. For example, if you are terrified of speaking, you are not going to be suddenly comfortable speaking in front of 3,000 people at a conference, are you?

The gap is too big. If you are starting from a place where you are shaking, and worrying if you can do it, it's not going to happen, or not very fast anyhow. It is a bit like driving a car with the brake on. Is it not going to be rather hard work? It doesn't have to be about speaking, it could be about doing something different, doing something new.

Changing jobs, going back to work after having a family, setting up a business, applying for a new job, settling in a new country. Life after redundancy, bereavement, illness, bankruptcy. It all knocks your confidence. How do you start or even **re**start?

You need to put in place all the little steps one by one until the business gets off the ground. If your goal is to present at a convention or do a presentation for your business, you need to work on the fear first, and little by little develop your confidence, "un petit pas," [one tiny step] at a time. You need to practise.

The first few times are not going to be great; you will make mistakes, you will stumble, you will shake and tremble but that is the beauty of it. You've never done that so it's a new start, a new skill.

I have been a teacher all my life, so being in front of a group is very natural to me. It's probably my best way of being because I'm so used to it. I'm completely in my element, it's part of me. But it wasn't like that when I started 20 years ago. It was very scary and holding the attention of 30 temperamental teenagers is a real challenge. I take my hat off to all the teachers who are still in full-time teaching; they are heroes! I had my own deep experience of fear about speaking, and it's why I help other people to speak today.

WHAT PEOPLE HAVE SAID ABOUT
HÉLÈNE'S COURSES

"Hélène is a trained teacher who specialised in drama. However she admits that as a teacher she was so scared of public speaking that she always avoided volunteering to run an assembly. Consequently, Hélène feels she was overlooked for opportunities as she was never brave enough to truly stand out.

A few of us had already done some training with Hélène over the last few weeks. This week I was thrilled to see how the women have looked so radiant and confident and willing to be vulnerable and share what is important to them. The sessions have certainly helped me feel easier in myself and then I can flow and enjoy myself more too!"

Rosemary Cunningham, Winning Women Essex Ambassador
See more at:
http://www.rosemarycunningham.co.uk/blog/public-speaking-made-easy

I really want you to think about the **little steps.** I want you to think about celebrating the little steps. The journey is rich, the journey is beautiful. Even if you are scared, your confidence will grow and you will feel good.

It's worth living through and enjoying. It's worth celebrating the first time you go to an event or a networking meeting and have the courage to say a few words, only a few to start with.

Being able to go to the shops and make a complaint and feel okay about it. (I wrote a whole section, how to get a tin of decking oil for free!) Being able to ask your boss for a pay rise because you know you deserve it. Being able to speak in front of your team without worrying what they think of you.

I heard this recently: *"What other people think about you is none of your business"*. My first reaction was *"But it IS about me and it IS my business"*. Actually NO, you do NOT need to know. Let's face it, there will be people who do not like you and that is fine, there will more people who do love you and these are the ones you have to focus on as they will bring you lots of support and happiness.

I have made a series of videos, and *"Rome was not built in a day"* is one of my favourite ones. Find it on my blog post.

http://www.Hélènemusso.com/acknowledging-the-little-steps/

4. Breathe!

Best
Balanced
Beautiful
Basic
Barmy
Buoyant
But
Bashful
and even
Bizarre

Breathing costs nothing and is always available, except maybe ...under water!

Let me introduce you to the power of YOUR breath.

Breathing is a natural process; we don't think about breathing. We are born with the ability to breathe. I believe we take 20,000 breaths a day in order to live, which is a huge amount of air going in and out. The air enters in an effortless manner into our lungs and meanwhile we rush around, get busy and ignore that powerful tool within us.

Actually, when you start expressing yourself, especially in public when you are nervous - because the attention is on you - you need to think about the breath and use it so that it is your ally, so that it supports you.

Often when you are speaking, you are likely to be standing and your whole body is engaged, and you need to engage your breath very quickly so your brain gets the maximum amount of oxygen for maximum performance. By taking some very long deep breaths before speaking, you will calm yourself, you will be more prepared and the increased levels of oxygen rushing to your brain will allow you to think more clearly and minimise the risk of your mind going blank or your body going into freeze mode.

Although this is not new - I am not reinventing the wheel here - a lot of people don't use it.

BE DIFFERENT; USE IT

It is free, it is simple and it is available. Under stress we centre the breath in our throat and upper body making it difficult for us to relax. You can learn very easily to reprogram or retune our brains to use the breath to your advantage.

Simple, fun and effective exercise:

Do it as often as you want/can/desire

Make it a **habit** and you will develop a more relaxed stance on life.

- Stand up and imagine you are making a speech in front of an audience
- Shake your body, roll your shoulders back and allow yourself to relax
- Take a deep, long breath in through your nose and out through your mouth. Most people will stiffen their shoulders at that point, rest your hand on your chest and ensure that your shoulders are relaxed.
- Start thinking about **Depth.** You need your breath to go down, down, down. Imagine you are in a lift in a skyscraper for example, and you and the lift are going down. The same must happen with your breath. Take it from the top of your nose, allow it to enter your chest, and then finally into your stomach which is where you want the air to go. It is a long journey all the way through your body. I call this the **long deep breath**.
- The air should stay in your stomach for a second or two, then as you exhale you will pull

your stomach in and the air will come out. It's important not to do it too fast, you may hyperventilate! Do this exercise with one hand on your chest and one hand on your stomach. You will feel the air fill your belly and then feel it being pushed out as you exhale. Do this at least **three times.** I hear you say *"But I'm just about to speak, to make a presentation, I can't do that in front of everyone!"* Of course not. But you can do it in the car, in the toilets, the lobby, anywhere that is calm and quiet, a little time on your own before you turn. It does not have to be big and dramatic, it can be done discreetly, but it is one **simple** secret **recipe for success**. Even if you are still nervous, you will be calmer.

I have a blog with a video if you prefer to hear and watch this exercise:
http://www.Hélènemusso.com/breathe-before-speaking-1-2-3/

Use the breath to your advantage. The breath is automatic, but if you **work with YOUR breath**, you will be on the road to success.

WHAT PEOPLE HAVE SAID ABOUT HÉLÈNE'S COURSES

"Hélène presents in a lively and captivating way displaying passion and belief in herself, transferring honest and positive energy. She radiates such positive energy which is impossible to avoid. It is externally very obvious when Hélène believes in/is connected to, whatever it is she is presenting to someone. For anyone wanting to develop and tune into such skills, she can help you "feel the fear and do it anyway"

Angela, student, Anglia Ruskin University

THE PRINCIPLES OF BEING KIND TO YOURSELF

-Rest
-Play
-Eat well every day
-Love yourself
-Love others
-Breathe
-Move
-No comparison to others
-Let go of judgement
-Dream
(on the island of La Reunion)

THE 5 KEYS TO UNLOCK YOUR
OUTRAGEOUS EXPRESSION

Part 3: Practise!

PRACTISE!

1. Take The Drama Out Of Practice!

Stop making a drama out of practice, stop being a drama queen, you will have to practice to get better, so just get on with it!

Practice is one of the keys to unlock your expression, your voice. Most of us want to bypass the practice, because we want instant results. Be different, do not shy away from practice. Be prepared to do and redo and do and redo and do and... It is never too late to learn and do and redo some exercises, be prepared to learn and relearn. Relish the learning.

How did you learn to walk? By falling and trying again, by falling and trying again. How did you learn to drive? By trying and driving, by trying and driving and driving some more. How did you learn your job? ...You can fill the gap yourself. Most of us think it is going to be "hard work" and then end up not doing any practice whatsoever.

Thinking back to the section on language, what would you be able to see if you changed the thought "hard work" to "a pleasant activity"? We also want instant results, instant gratification and we do not allow ourselves to learn. Remind yourself that Rome was not built in a day. Allow time to be your ally, your companion, and value the process instead of aiming for the results.

That is the reason why I run workshops as they give you the platform to practice in a safe and supportive environment and just practice. In this day and age of information overload, where we can learn so much by watching and reading on the internet, I still believe that we need to be given **an exclusive place to express ourselves**, away from the everyday and the busyness of life, a training ground before the big day, whether the big day is an actual presentation or being able to complain in a shop for damaged goods. When are you starting then?

Practice is about the **courage** to try, to try again and again and to fail. Without failure there is no feedback, so be prepared to learn with the acceptance of the little steps. Take risks and **be proud for trying and having a voice.**

A STORY FROM THE PAST

Today, I worked with a group of Winning Women, a business networking group from Leigh on Sea. Some had already worked with me, others had not. What they all had in common was an anxiety ranging from 3 to 8 - on my anxiety scale - about having to make a speech in public to the main Winning Women group next week.

I am a real advocate of creating a safe environment in which speaking and expressing yourself can flourish. Because, consider this, if you are not respected, feel you are not heard and not listened to, how are you going to be open and open up to others? If you are petrified because you think others are going to judge anything and everything you do and say, how can you find your own unique voice? Can you really?

I remember sitting in meetings with my peers as a teacher, holding my tongue because I felt that my contribution might be seen as arrogance. As a drama teacher, there were a lot of interesting and creative ideas that we used every day in the drama classroom which frightened the hell out of the other teachers. So I was often held back by fear of being ostracised, rejected and considered as a smart "a", if you see my meaning. Now I wish I had had the courage to have my say without fear as I think respect would have come out of it and it would have given me more credibility and more confidence.

Now I am not afraid anymore.

I know I have value to offer and I am getting my own confidence when I see others blossoming and opening up.

Here we were today, all business women, each with a big heart full of love and desire to give and to teach and to contribute to other people's lives through our business. But before you can sell your products, you need to have the confidence to talk about it and believe that you can, in a small space, with others who can support you.

What makes a difference is my unshakable belief that we can all have a voice. By the end of the session, I could feel happiness in the room, a sense of "I can" instead of "I can't", and a renewed confidence. And you know what? We should be so grateful to the Miller and Carter pub on the Rayleigh road for trusting us to just create magic in their pub!

In a nutshell
- **Consider practice essential**
- **Make practice a pleasurable activity**
- **Allow time to develop**
- **Enjoy the process**
- **Find places you can practise - of course my workshops, but not exclusively - I am one of the answers, not all the answers!**

Go to http://www.hélènemusso.co.uk/courses

WHAT PEOPLE HAVE SAID ABOUT HÉLÈNE'S COURSES

"Thank you Hélène Musso for today, I attended Public Speaking Demystified level one, I really enjoyed the day great group and a fab trainer, really enjoyed your training techniques and I will look forward to putting those into practice. Anyone that's a bundle of nerves like me speaking do see Hélène."

Andrea Hall

"I learned so much from Hélène and it is largely because of her that I am able to run my own events and feel comfortable speaking, which is something I never imagined would happen."

"When I first attended one of Hélène's short courses I was nervous even to stand in front of the group to speak. I had been trained in advocacy for my profession but speaking from the heart was something different! In a couple of hours Hélène showed me how to connect with an audience and gave me the confidence I needed to make a start.

Later, I attended a one day course with Hélène which really helped me to build a solid foundation. I learned to deliver my message and to feel confident before an audience. The experience was fun and inspiring and I felt comfortable in the safe space that Hélène held for us.

I was also lucky enough to experience a transformational afternoon during which Hélène coached me in speaking in front of a camera. I went from awkward to poised in a few short hours and a whole world of new possibilities opened up for me. I now have the confidence to host my own events, to grasp with both hands any opportunities to speak no matter how large the audience, and I have the wonderful gift of knowing that public speaking can be enjoyable and fulfilling, rather than terrifying. Thanks, Hélène!"

Harriet Balcombe, Mind Calm coach

2 Take risks

Have a look at this beautiful spiral stairs and picture yourself going down the stairs, slowly one step at the time. No problem.

Now imagine that you are being chased by a stranger who wants to harm you and you have to run downstairs. Getting scary now, is it not?

Now you carry on running and you realise that the only way you are going to escape from this unpleasant character is by jumping down the middle of the stairs. Look at it, can you see the bottom? No, it is a bit too dark. Your heart is pounding and you want to scream. Can you do it, can you trust and speed up your pace? Or are you still too high and may you hurt yourself?

Sometimes, in life we have to jump, not physically but metaphorically. We have to take the first step then the second one and then suddenly we have to go.

In 2007 I went white water rafting in Switzerland. I was enjoying the water, the people and it was fun. At some point we moored the boats and climbed on a rock. *"What we are going to do,"* explained our guide, *"is to jump from here, into the water and then you need to make sure you keep your body straight and let the current lead you."*

I am a very good swimmer but the jump terrified me and I started making excuses that I might hurt myself, that I was scared, and that I could not do it. Before I had time to properly protest, our guide took my hand kindly but firmly and said *"Ladies first!"* and, suddenly, I was flying in the air.

I gracefully fell in the water and let the current take me with glee. His hand was all it took - and trust from the guide that I could do it. I needed some support but not much and I especially did not need to start a battle of negative thoughts going round my head. I did not have time and I was beaming by the time I went back on the boat.

I am not talking about major risks here - unless you like extreme sports. I am more describing an **attitude to life t**o help you to come out of your shell and become a more outrageous confident individual. For example, I do not think I will ever jump off a plane, not necessarily because I am scared - maybe a little bit in all fairness - but more because that does not interest me enough. Climbing Machu Picchu and going trekking in Nepal sounds much more interesting, or, climbing the hills and mountains of La Reunion in the Indian Ocean any day too!

We are all very confident in some areas and less confident in others. We often **take for granted what we know** and what is easy for us and **brand ourselves as failures** if we attempt to learn a new skill and give up before we have had any time to master it!

A STORY FROM THE PAST: RISK AND CHANGING YOUR PERSPECTIVE ON THE EVENTS OF YOUR LIFE

Like every teenager, I was desperate to fit in but did not ever really manage to. I was popular enough at school but never in the "IN" crowd and not quite sure I wanted to be. Most teenagers at the time of my adolescence in France hung around with their roaring mopeds and talking about very little. This looked and sounded far too tedious to me. The few times I joined in, I felt silly, under scrutiny and really trying too hard to be cool. So I distanced myself.

I wish now I had been in a sporty group with a common goal but I was not competitive and not interested in winning. It is ironic that I am now supporting a networking business group called Winning Women and they are fab!

I also liked activities which did not appeal to other teenagers like singing in choirs, where my own sense of belonging was very strong through music. Obviously, if you tell your peers that your best kick at 15 is to sing in a folk choir, they think you are a weirdo. This was definitely not cool like the X factor culture.

I also discovered that I was attractive to boys, but this only massaged my ego for years. I did not see much point in getting attached with so many fish in the sea! I spent a lot of time breaking hearts, and potentially damaging mine. Undermining my own efforts to find someone remotely suitable for years.

So at 20, although in perfect health and studying hard for two degrees, I was scolding myself inside and was unable to really reach out to people or find a real sense of direction. In my case, I chose what I call the easy option but for others and most would consider an act of courage - I left France.

Yes, I left everything behind and moved to England. I only intended it to be temporary originally, to learn English. Strangely enough I considered this move to be an act of cowardice. As I could not fit in in my own country, I may as well see if I could fit in somewhere else. Incidentally, I also had my eyes set on America but it was too far away, too strange, too foreign and the French are overall quite anti-American and I thought this was going to be far too difficult. So I chose England.

Many years later I realised that this ability to leave is actually very courageous. If everything else fails in my life, I leave. I have left relationships, jobs and *friends and realise that often by leaving I create a better reality for myself. **I also discovered that you can be happy anywhere as long as you believe you can.** I go on holidays and I love it. I live in England and I love it. I go to see a friend and I love it. I do the washing up and I love it - maybe not as much in this case! But you get my gist!*

*It is not what happens to you which makes a difference to your life but **how you react to it,** what your response is. If your car breaks down and you start to panic and think that the world is against you, then it is hard to bear.*

However, if you consider that maybe your car is old and you have never ever spent much money on a service, then it is time to say goodbye to the car. It is therefore not as hard to cope with the break down.

Time to Play

From a big risk to a small risk

- Think about a skill or just something you have not been able to achieve but would love to.
- Now think about something that is so easy for you and compare them: What is the difference?
- What is a big risk to you?
- What seems a big risk to you will be easy for others. You can only start **where you are**. If it is an achievement for you to open your front door and go outside then start there. If it means joining a club so that you keep the loneliness at bay, start there. If it is taking a plane without feeling scared then do it. **Start where you are, do not let anyone decide for you and let go of judgment.**
- Look around for others who have the skills the attitudes, the qualities you desire, watch them, hang around them, listen to them, talk to them, immerse yourself and be open to novelty! Children learn like that and pick up some of our good and bad habits and you can do the same as an adult!

A STORY FROM THE PAST: ABOUT RISK

In 2007, I was returning from travelling in France with my new born baby. I took the ferry with my car. I was determined to have a nice meal so splashed out on a lovely lunch in the French restaurant on board. I was happy but alone (apart from my obvious pushchair and adorable baby).

I had noticed a guy looking at me a few times but did not think much of it. At the end of the trip, as I was getting inside my car, I noticed a Porsche parked in front of me. I admired it for an instant but soon my mind wandered in other directions again. I am not that materialistic and cars are mainly tools to get me from A to B.

I realised as I put a foot (or more like tyre) in England that I needed some petrol and stopped at the first available petrol station. After I had paid for my petrol, I noticed next to my car the Porsche from the ferry. The owner of the car was filling up and turned towards me. We exchanged a few polite words and he looked at me and then said, "Here is my number, contact me sometime, if you like." and put a crumpled piece of paper in my hand. I was rather surprised then drove off.

A few weeks later, I contacted that guy, David, and for several years he became a very good friend. We went to Bilbao and Berlin as well as skiing twice. We met for meals and outings and travelled to Cornwall too.

*Although I have not seen David now for a few years, I had taken the **risk** to phone him without knowing anything else and from there a friendship had developed and with it some wonderful times to remember. We chatted a lot and really understood each other and gave each other much support for those few years and, for that, I am happy I did not throw away the crumpled piece of paper that he put in my hand the day I met him.*

Key rules to take risks

○   Take **calculated** risks (prepare yourself physically for a marathon or a bungee jump, for example)

○   I think that everyone starts with positive intentions, so I trust that they are going to be trustworthy and kind. If you hold that as a belief, you very rarely get into difficult situations.

○   Trust but **look after yourself**; meet people in public places for example when you do not know them. Please do not walk into an unknown city at night alone.

o   *You* have to **take some action**, even if you are scared as nobody is going to do it for you. Pick up the phone and talk to a complete stranger, find the courage to talk to this beautiful lady or man who stands, every morning, on the same platform as you.

The more you take risks, the easier it becomes, the less you take risks, the more your life shrinks, take the first step!

<u>SAFETY AND RISKS</u>

I believe we can only take risks if we feel safe enough to take that risk. Safety is first and then risk second. I do not believe that we learn anything of value, apart from being traumatised, if we are thrown into the lion's den. Some people might disagree with me and I wish them well. The aim of my work is to make sure YOU feel very safe.

If you come to my courses, you will play, participate and learn, even if you are scared. I am just asking you to try, to give it a go, to surprise yourself and to just be yourself and have fun!

Risk is subjective; do not compare yourself to others. *Comparison erosion is likely to make you feel even smaller.* The individuals who appear the most successful also have their own problems! This is very hard to see when you feel down.

Best tip: Switch off Facebook when you feel low; other people's wonderful stories can make you feel unwell. Resource yourself and then you can hear them again later on. Believe me; you have not missed anything!

TAKING RISKS: MINI GUIDE ON TALKING TO COMPLETE STRANGERS

What's the point?

We are social animals, we need other people to thrive.

New people means new ventures.

Making connections is fun.

Making connections means finding support and friendship, sometimes love.

A STORY FROM THE PAST: AT SPITALFIELDS MARKET.

A while ago, I was on a course next to Spitalfields market in East London. It has become a very trendy area and it is heaving with people, stalls, traders and tourists. Under the main covered market, there are long benches and tables. Quite by accident you could end up eating the food you have purchased onsite facing a complete stranger.

The course encouraged my extrovert nature and I exchanged some banter with the stall seller when I bought my lunch. Soon, I am sitting down facing a beautiful but forlorn lady who appeared sad and lonely. She had large golden earrings and I struck up a conversation. I found out she was from Tenerife and was struggling with learning English. She told me that she found being in a language class full of very young people very difficult. I could empathise - as I had been in that same position many years ago - and I purposefully articulated every word and slowed down my usual fast speaking pace to help her converse with me.

When she left, she was replaced with a fair young-looking lady with colourful clothes, large glasses with a long chain attached to them and looking slightly eccentric.

Her nails were curiously painted but with different colours which made it rather cute and funny. She was eating a wrap, which isn't the easiest thing to eat tidily in front of a complete stranger, but I thought nevertheless she's in front of me, so I will talk to her.

I was trying to make eye contact but she was engrossed in her eating, and she was not returning my gaze. So I used the nails to make contact and said: "You have lovely nails", with a light hearted tone in my voice. She immediately beamed and responded and I started asking her questions about her life.

She was bubbly and talked fast. What I marvelled at is not my conversation with her but the fact that our discussion was soon interrupted by interested parties next to us. As the girl was working at the Psychedelic society, she had strong opinions about drug use. The couple next to us had personal and professional interest in that discussion. I soon lost track of the conversation which had gone beyond my actual understanding but I was happy to have been the go-between between two parties who had somehow a lot in common and wanted to have a debate on the issue. I left them as they exchanged email addresses, happy to have had a facilitating role and leaving for a stroll to look around.

Outrageous tips on meeting new people

Those who have seen me training know how it looks and feel effortless and I am able to respond and interact with my participants effectively and easily, what I call "thinking on my feet." This effortless way of being comes from trial and error in the classroom when I started teaching, where careful planning and preparation made a huge amount of difference to a lesson.

The outrageous tips below may feel very false to you and calculated but actually it can soon become second nature to you too. I simply deconstructed my strategy to make it available to YOU. Play with it and use it for YOU.

- In a public place, identify a place where it would easy to talk to someone for example, the benches of my story were perfect, a market stall with people looking at the same items, in a queue for food. The possibilities are endless but make it easy for yourself to reach to a complete stranger.

- Set yourself the intention of meeting someone, even if it is only for a brief interaction. Set the intention but let go of the HOW; there is no right or wrong here.
- Make sure you are neither tired or worried about your own problems.
- If you get scared, go for a walk first at a good pace to shake the cobwebs away!
- Once you have found a person you would like to talk to, then:
- Identify a feature of that person's body that you would like to comment on (ha,ha, very funny, nothing rude here, otherwise you will get a slap) a scarf, a pair of earrings, a colourful top, a ring...
- Make a simple comment, such as, *"I like your scarf, it is very pretty."*
- Make sure you make eye contact at the same time.
- Smile too!
- The rest will come: If you hear an accent, an easy question is *"Where are you from?"* If you are dealing with a British person ask, *"Which part of the country are you from?"*

If you get stuck, smile more and use the market stall as something to talk about.

In another encounter, I helped a tourist choose a piece of jewellery for his girlfriend as he was indecisive and I made a few suggestions to help him choose.

- A few seconds with no words is good and might mean you either need to move on or that the other person needs to ponder their answers. Either way, wait a few more seconds before deciding to leave or persevere.

I often finish, *"It was nice meeting you, what's your name?"*. Most people will give me their right hand to shake and, with a smile, tell me their name. Make sure you make eye contact several times during the interaction.

I challenge you to try this exercise and to get in touch with me on Facebook on "Public Speaking Demystified - Tame the fear" page with what you discover. Anyone who does will get entered for a half-price prize draw for one of my courses!

So what are you waiting for?

OUTRAGEOUSLY DARING: HOW TO COMPLAIN AND NEARLY ALWAYS GET YOUR OWN WAY

Like many people, I have an area of decking in my garden. The decking was getting green and grey and I knew I had to revamp it. I asked a few friends for advice and settled on cleaning it thoroughly with a special cleaner and then varnishing it with decking oil.

I went to the local DIY shop and bought a large tin of Ronseal Natural cedar oil. I also bought the brush and handle suggested for that purpose.

The description for coverage was as follow; "This 5 Litre pack is normally sufficient to coat 20-24 m^2 with 2 coats. Coverage will vary with absorbency of timber and profile of deck." Aware that my decking was around 12 to 15 m^2, I calculated that I had more than enough with only one large tin of the product.

I dithered for weeks. Then my friend Paul kindly offered his help and we started to paint! Unfortunately, we out of the Ronseal oil with only half the decking covered. It was a summer Sunday evening and there was no way we could buy some more. I decided to "complain" the following day. Now, just in the word "complain", there is this unpleasant feeling that you have to argue, put your foot down and maybe scream. However, I am a coach and this is not the mode I want to operate in. After all, I am a coach, let's use what I have learnt. So I arrived with my empty tin with two things in my head, I want to get another tin for free or half price and I want to do it in a polite and respectful manner.

The first lady I encountered was a pretty, blond middle aged lady who was serving on the Customer Service desk and spoke slowly. I put down my empty tin and set to explain, in my direct and precise mode. She very quickly asked me: "Have you taken photos?" questioning whether or not I was lying. At that point, I paused, looked her straight in the eyes and replied, "I am acting in good faith" and re-explained the sequence of events.

I could see she was puzzled and she very quickly added, "I am not going to say I am an expert in this product and the use of the product, I would be lying if I did that," looking at the tin as if it had magic powers. She then suggested. "I will find someone from the paint department for you."

She sent out a message over the public address system and soon after that, a brunette lady appeared looking a bit hassled and tired. That lady did listen and empathise but thought as it is Ronseal and not them producing the product there was not very much they could do. I disagreed and talked about quality assurance. It was obvious she could not do much and she acknowledged that and suggested I talked to the duty manager.

I smiled and thanked her for response and asked then for the duty manager. He arrived within five minutes but it felt like eternity as I was standing there waiting for him and smiling sheepishly to other customers.

But to my delight, once he arrived, he openly agreed with me and I got just what I had gone in there for - a tin of decking oil at half price!

There are some lessons in this:

- ☐ *Set your intentions beforehand - in my case get a tin of decking oil for free or half price - and keep calm.*
- ☐ *Be prepared for some waiting time.*
- ☐ *Be prepared to repeat the same story, play the broken record - it is a technique that teachers use all the time when children are not compliant.*

☐ *Be honest and complain only if it is the manufacturer/producer's fault.*

☐ *Be clear and re-explain the same story.*

☐ *Be considerate to the employees, say thank you for their time.*

☐ *Be prepared to talk to the manager, someone in charge who has authority to offer a refund or a discount.*

☐ *Smile.*

☐ *Say thank you and mean it, not just 'lip service'. Even if I had not been able to get what I wanted I think it is important to thank people for listening and attempting to help you. It does not hurt anyone and makes most people happy, including yourself!*

THE 5 KEYS TO UNLOCK YOUR
OUTRAGEOUS EXPRESSION

Part 4: Have Fun!

HAVE FUN!

Having fun is a serious business.

If you only work and have little fun in your life or you get yourself sucked in the mundanity of life and the pettiness of everyday, then you are missing out. Most importantly, it has been proven now that playing and having fun, not only makes us happier but also relieves stress, and allows us to work much more effectively, establish better relationships with others and improve our brain function.

Which brain would you prefer?
This one?

Or this one?

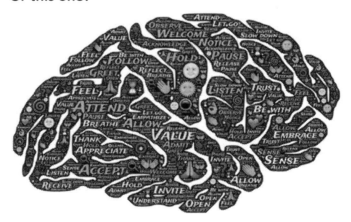

And for an oldie like me, it keeps us much much younger. A bit like this:

"We don't stop playing because we grow old; we grow old because we stop playing."

George Bernard Shaw

Playing comes in different shapes and forms, it can be spontaneous or organised and it can be a one-off or a regular occurrence. This will depend on your state of mind and your time and willingness to explore. I have fun just sitting at a café observing how people interact and create mini-stories about their lives. However, I would not want to do that all the time. I have fun running every Saturday with ParkRun in my local park and this fun is more organised and pre-planned.

What I strongly believe is you can only have fun if you are fully present. **Fun** here does not mean just a quick moment of laughter but **a real awareness of grasping life with both hands and experiencing every minute with an ever increasing light-hearted way of being.**

1: Be Present

Be present - or practice presence - What does this actually mean?

This is difficult to explain but I can summarise it as: **Once you have decided to be somewhere, give it 100% a**nd *commit yourself fully to the place, space and people.* Essentially, do not be half-hearted. You actually waste more energy.

For example, there is no point going to a party thinking, *"I am not going to have a good time"* or *"I will only stay for an hour because I have to"*. You may as well commit, surrender and give it your best. What is then likely to happen is that you will enjoy anything and everyone who comes your way during that time!

A STORY FROM THE PAST: ON BEING PRESENT

As a coach I go to other workshops to get inspired, refresh my own skills or learn some new ones. I went to a confidence-building course using drama and improvisation recently. The experience was amazing and it brought to the surface aspects I had never thought about before! One was on being fully present.

If I am IN the room, am I not present enough? In school we answer "present" when the teacher calls the register so that she knows we are 'physically' in the room. But what about our minds and spirits, are they really present? What happens when you feel you would rather be somewhere else? What happens if you are too tired and you do not have the energy to be involved? What happens if your mind is worrying about work, the kids, the washing the cleaning, the bills the...?

Aaaargh!

Being present is allowing yourself to be physically in the room and also engage your mind fully. Being present is about grasping and grabbing the present moment and making the most of it, entirely, completely.

I used to go to staff training thinking "What are they going to tell me that I do not know already?" What a waste of time; I'd rather finish my marking!" With such an attitude, I never really learnt much from other people's training simply because I was not present enough.

As an adult you have a choice, you could potentially walk out of the room, so before you enter the room, just ask yourself softly: "Do I want to be here? Do I really want to?" If you do, make yourself the promise to get involved fully and completely. **Story to be continued...**

BEING PRESENT AT YOUR OFFICE: A REFLECTIVE GAME

Now let's look at your work, if every morning you enter your office, and the only urge you have is to walk out and go somewhere else, below are some questions you need to ask:

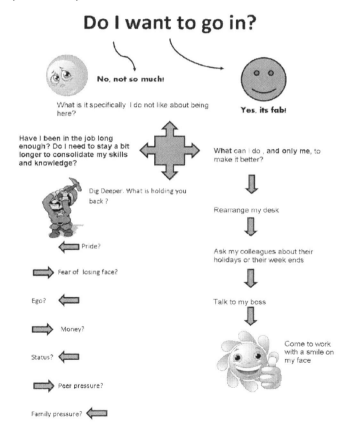

Do I want to go in?

No, not so much!

What is it specifically I do not like about being here?

Have I been in the job long enough? Do I need to stay a bit longer to consolidate my skills and knowledge?

Dig Deeper. What is holding you back?

Pride?

Fear of losing face?

Ego?

Money?

Status?

Peer pressure?

Family pressure?

Yes, its fab!

What can I do, and only me, to make it better?

Rearrange my desk

Ask my colleagues about their holidays or their week ends

Talk to my boss

Come to work with a smile on my face

BEST TIPS ON BEING PRESENT: GET MOVING!

STORY CONTINUING...

Let's go back to the workshop I had attended: so there I am in the room. I have managed to overcome why I am here; I have walked in the room but I underestimated how the physicality of the course would have a beneficial impact on my overall mood, attitude and interaction with others.

The course was physically demanding because we had to move a lot and "play the fool". In other words we played a range of characters. As the work was improvised and spontaneous, you could only respond in the moment, again, by being present. Being in the present meaning purely: we get out of our heads and let our bodies take over. We are one body and one mind and we are whole and complete.

One participant explained that when she moves, she feels completely in the present and that is the reason why any type of physical activity is good but the trick is to find one physical activity that you really enjoy, you really have fun with and it will be different for all of us. NEVER ever choose an activity because you have to, as you will give up very quickly. Choose an activity which makes you so engrossed you lose any notion of time and space and your whole focus is on that movement, on that effort, on that rush of adrenalin into your body.

During this course, it was suggested that we carry on being present in our lunch break and it became about raising our own awareness. At the moment my awareness is very visual. In my newly found awareness, I just constantly look around at everyone and everything. It is a bit like a horse when its blinkers are removed. Suddenly I can really see. It is a very odd but empowering feeling.

What is most enlightening is that I thoroughly engage with my surroundings. As a youngster I very rarely looked at signs above shops. My memories are based on a vague feeling of non-engagement or cool detachment in which everything appears undefined as if coated with a permanent grey mist. I'm not afraid anymore to make regular eye contact with people and to smile. This new attitude is also coupled with an increased need for looking after my health and eating/sleeping/drinking properly so that I can feel on top of my world.

To get back to the course. I had a dip in the early afternoon as I became so hungry, I started feeling unwell. This brings me to remind you to make sure you replenish your batteries and you get food and rest. How many of us are sleep deprived and eat so quickly that we have little understanding of the food we gobble down our throats?

Allow yourself time to just stop, contemplate what you really want to eat and doze off in the comfort of a nice armchair or a bed for a well-deserved afternoon nap. In order to be fully in the present, you have to make sure you fulfil your basics needs, food, water, and shelter and not skip these essentials.

2. Discover your fun!

We have been told how to have fun, at certain times and with certain rules and under the diktat of society. In Western society, we are conditioned as follows: all week we work and we are not allowed much fun. We are working, so we cannot have any fun, of course not! Or if we are, it will mean dealing with a hangover the following day.

Work is supposed to be a very serious activity and we take ourselves too seriously when working. When one listens to some radio stations, it feels like we are only waiting for Friday night to get drunk, dance and have fun, and the weekend is the only way to think about fun after a week of sadness, drudgery and utter boredom.

A STORY FROM THE PAST: ABOUT HAVING FUN.

I used to believe that this was the only way to live. Waiting impatiently for the weekend to make up for the lack of fun during the week, up to the point where you are not present during the week and you feel utterly detached from reality. After a few years in teaching, I was exhausted by the demands of the job, and bored by the routine of school. So I started living for weekends and especially for the holidays.

I reminded myself of my miserable existence every minute of the day, just to be relieved momentarily by the fact that it is difficult to teach without being fully present.

After adopting such a negative attitude, I very soon realised that if I was not going to change something, I would be slowly dying inside; a small emotional death. So, in Hélène's style, I left. I worked for a year as a recruitment consultant, realised that the grass was not always greener on the other side and went back... to teaching.

The difference was that I decided then I would teach on my own terms. As it happens, part-time teaching and a temporary contract meant that for several years I could keep my health, my sanity, some income, and I did not have time to get sucked up into the politics of an institution. It was not perfect but it suited me with a young child in tow.

So what has this got to do with fun? In my case the lack of balance between work-life and personal/ social-life meant that I could not express myself and find a happy medium. I was not having fun. By choosing a new way of working and accepting that not everything is set in stone forever, I created a new reality which was closer to my needs.

Having fun also means reminding ourselves of being creative. We are all different and what is creative for one might be the very uncreative for others. What about using **pictures** to get you in the flow. Let's have fun! The photo above has a medieval feel. The sun is streaming through the opening and it is a nice spring day. Where are you? Where would you want to be? And most importantly what or who is behind that door?

Create your **own story** either by writing it or by drawing it. What is beyond the castle door? If you would prefer to record the story, use your phone and then post your creation on my Facebook page - Hélène Musso - or on "Public Speaking Demystified - Tame the Fear."

Prizes to be won of course!
We are playing after all!

Having fun for me means eating well and my absolute favourite food is a prawn salad. You may not like prawns yourself but look at the beauty of food and how inviting it is and colourful, (if this book was not in black and white due to my modest budget you would understand). I hope you come to my courses so that I can treat you to a book with colour pictures next time! ☺☺

Would you prefer this one? And before you worry about putting on weight and think "I am being bad today", just enjoy and admire it!

The first year I was living in England, a frequent question came up: "Do you miss France?" I used to reply "I miss speaking French and I miss the bakeries, the Boulangerie-Patisseries". It was definitely not because I might be a bread and cake addict. I preferred cheese at that time! The windows had the most exquisite cake displays which used to awaken my artistic side. I loved, and still do love, appreciating elaborate compositions and exhibits of culinary elegance. **Creativity pairs up with beauty.**

Nothing outrageous there is just common sense!

To recap - a summary on having fun!

- ☺ Be present
- ☺ Look after yourself - basic needs: water, food and a safe place to rest/live.
- ☺ Are you having fun reminder system - Ask yourself: am I having fun? If not, what can I do to make it different?
- ☺ Play, find one or several activities to make you play, whether it is tinkering with an old car or playing pool with friends
- ☺ Dance or another activity which makes you happy but makes you move. Please do not tell me you cannot, I work with people with physical disabilities and they can move one way or another!
- ☺ Move even more!
- ☺ Find fun in the details of everyday life!

FUN FILLER OR FUN FULL STOP

Using the **frames** in the following pictures, find some felt-tip pens to colour the frame and draw or paint or sketch **your future, your desires, your wishes, your ideal world, your friends,** and so on - your life in a nutshell or the one which you desire.

What would YOU like to see here?

What is in the frame?

Can you colour these houses to match your dreams?

Where does this doorway lead you?

ON FUN!

When was the last time you played a good game of blowing bubbles or just observing the lights in the bubbles? Observe the picture below if not. Then do it in your garden even if you do not have children!

We all find fun in different activities. I have two visitors at the moment and they are both into cooking. One prepares very healthy lunches and meals for himself with fragrant fresh herbs.

The other one is captivated by the latest dish brought by a Mediterranean cook, Yotam

Ottolenghi and so experiments with various recipes.

He admitted a while ago after a stressful time at work locking himself in his kitchen and spending four days just cooking and cooking and cooking.

Whilst their attention to food is a bit beyond me, as I prefer eating nice food than making it, they are obviously having fun in the preparing, the cooking and the tasting. I cannot wait for our next dinner!

ALLOWING OTHERS TO HAVE FUN.

What is fun for me is not going to be necessarily fun for anyone else. If you are a couple or a family, this is paramount to respect and understanding. You cannot control everything and why would you want to anyhow? Letting go will allow you and others to be more happy and for everyone to do what they really want to do. It becomes a win/win situation.

THE 5 KEYS TO UNLOCK YOUR OUTRAGEOUS EXPRESSION

Part 5:Discover Your Extraordinary Story.

DISCOVER YOUR EXTRAORDINARY STORY

Or find out what your extraordinary story is!

How to uncover your Outrageous and extraordinary story? I often hear, "I do not have one, I have just led a simple life." Yes, this is true - we do live mundane lives but we also do things which are extraordinary.

Do you know why you do not think it is extraordinary? It's simply because our stories are part of us and we take them for granted. We do what we do and never really think that it can be extraordinary.

We see it in other people. Any of you who secretly wanted to be like your best friend because she/he had the qualities you did not feel you had? You may find out that someone else wishes they had yours. I am quite a nervous person and get agitated when under pressure and I really admire calm people because they seem to cope better with life.

1. What is the point of discovering your extraordinary story?

I would reply: What is the point of life?

You only have one life and if you do not make it yours then who else is going to do it?

- ☐ It will increase your self-esteem. My discovery over filling a piece of paper - applying for the threshold payment - which is a way to earn more money as a teacher, allowed me to value the huge contribution I had made to the school I was working for in at the time.
- ☐ It will allow you to take stock and think - do I want to carry on like this? Am I enjoying what I do?
- ☐ It will help you to regain control by asking "How much input have I got in my life?" "How can I shape my life so I feel empowered instead of being subjected to it?" There is no need to feel like a victim.
- ☐ It will help to access the next step and identify forthcoming steps.
- ☐ It will make you interesting to others if you share the story about your business or your work.

Be careful not to undermine yourself at any time: I went to a networking evening some time go and I heard several times things like, "Oh I am just…", "Oh, I just do…". "Oh, I merely…". What a way to introduce yourself! Whether you are a man, woman, single man or married you are making a contribution to others all the time , by just by being!

Allow yourself to be **vulnerable**; that is the hardest part. Most of us think it is a weakness to show our real self and to admit what we have done or to acknowledge our mistakes.

Outrageous tip:

Prepare your own funeral. That might sound rather morbid. But on your deathbed, how would you like to be remembered?

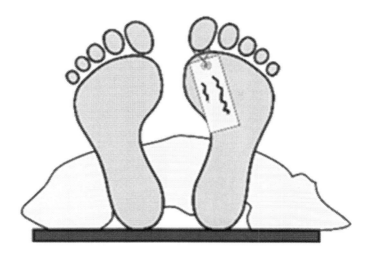

My friend Michele said: "I do not want to be remembered for having kept my house clean but for having being able to be a good friend". And a good friend she is.

Write your own eulogy or funeral speech: I know I want to be remembered for being full of life, confident, courageous, inspirational, mad, eccentric, fiercely resourceful, passionate, beautiful and sexy. Why not? And also for the years of helping others to uncover themselves, reengage, rediscover and fall back in love with life!

Outrageous Tip:

Pick one moment in your life which was important to you, then pick precise memories of that moment that you can see, hear and feel.

What do you remember, which colours do you see, which sounds do you hear, who was there with you? You need to visualise, hear and smell and feel the memory so that it becomes vivid. Now tell a friend about that memory, making sure you refer to all your senses.

You do not have to have travelled the world, earned lots of money and lived in a mansion to have an extraordinary story. Your story starts with your being born and making a contribution to the world, to your friends, to your colleagues, to your family.

I used to think that what I *did* was my only contribution to society. Now that I accept myself much more, I know that my contribution at times is just being me and inspiring others. I do not do very much, I just *am*. Once you have realised that you have to stop trying so hard and let it happen and to trust, then you start to see this extraordinary story of yours.

3. The extraordinary story of a self-confessed introvert who managed to reach out!

In 2014, I met Cristina Alciati, an Italian girl passionate about sport and fitness and very shy in nature. We became friends and this is her story, from the heart.

I [Cristina] became a business owner mostly by accident and with just a vague plan in the beginning that was more along the lines of "if this happens then perhaps I could do this and that"... and when the "this" happened I found myself with the perfect opportunity to have a go at doing "this and that". I wouldn't recommend this approach to everyone as it can lead you down a path of anxiety and frustration, however it's in my nature to push my boundaries and venture out in territories that are new to me and, even if I am very vocal about my disappointments, I not only survive but thrive from adversity so this is how I did it.

*One of the episodes that I remember most fondly was the first time **I utilised the power of the***

***internet to reach out to people whom I shared an
interest in horses with****. This must have been some
twenty years ago. It wasn't long before I was given
horse number 1 as a gift and had just met horse
number 2. Animals, like people, have all sorts of
issues and at the time I was spending every spare
moment studying, learning and researching their
behavioural habits and their wellbeing.*

*I also discovered the first internet forums on all
things equestrian. Somehow I bumped into this
forum where there were a lot of heated discussions
going on and two people stood out for me: one was
Paula, a feisty lady from Portugal who speaks
Italian better than me and who is a world famous
equestrian photographer and journalist. The other
one was Susan, a British lady living in Florence with
a long life passion for horses and on a quest to try
to educate people about the kinder ways of dealing
with horses and looking after their welfare as living
creatures as opposed to toys and objects with
which to show off.*

*Following a heated discussion on the forum about
saddle fitting I reached out to Susan to offer my
moral support and discuss my saddlers at the time.
This led to an exchange of emails over a period of a
few years and also gave me the courage to offer my*

opinion on the equestrian forum (I am an introvert and I don't talk to people just because they are there) which put me a little bit at odds with Paula and fanned the flames further.

Not budging from my position on the subject actually brought Paula and me closer and we started talking to each other and to share our experiences and values. We became friends and we still are to this day. I had the opportunity to learn to write for magazines exploring different writing styles and this eventually gave me the chance to express my own voice writing articles.

Roll forward a few years and after a change in jobs I ended up working in an office located near my local motorbike shop. During that time I made a couple of new friends and eventually I ended up going back to my roots as a motorcyclist from when I was a young teenager in Italy. I bought a big bike on Ebay. When I took it for an MOT it transpired that the reason for failing was that it missed some kind of link that operated the brake light.

This was 14+ years ago, Google was still in its infancy, a lot of businesses still didn't grasp the importance of being found on the internet and my beautiful motorbike was a model that was made exclusively for the Canadian market in 1985. Finding parts for it wasn't easy.

I followed the suggestion from a friend and joined the Owners' Club for that specific type of bike and started to discuss all things motorbike with other members when the owner announced that he was going to stop running the "club" because he had different interests and would be happy to give it to anyone wishing to continue with it. Nobody came forward and so I asked what the task entailed, just out of curiosity. The owner replied letting me know that I was the new owner of the club, waved goodbye and left.

I really had no clue on what to do but with a strong sense of adventure, a wicked sense of humour and somehow innate leadership qualities, I got the project off the ground.

I did what I thought would bring people a bit of relief from the struggles of everyday life and office politics when interacting on the forum and within six months of me taking over we had our first "in person" meeting at the legendary Ace Café in London which attracted a large number of members from all over the UK.

A few months later we attended the first of many rallies in the UK, and within a year we attended our first international rally in the Netherlands. Not long after that we started to organise our own events. Within the space of one or maybe two years membership numbers grew from just over 100 to several thousands of people from all over the world sharing their stories on the forum, exchanging banter and insults probably in equal measures, exchanging tips for modifications and so on... and it all started because I couldn't find a spare part to fix my bike.

I think this was probably the first time ever in my life that I found myself in a position of leadership with large numbers of people looking at me for direction and set to boundaries. According to some of the members I did a sterling job, others will say I am an idiot but then again if you don't get insults and detractors it means you are not doing a good enough job at leading your tribe.

Fast forward another 10 years or so and another aspect of my life took centre stage: health and fitness. After a lot of searching I found a pole dancing school in Southend and arranged my taster session. Because I was still fit from doing martial arts I cracked it and within 20 minutes I was hanging upside down. That's when I decided to make this a regular thing.

I didn't like the idea of sharing a pole with lots of other people so I searched for a better option. I bumped into the website of the reigning British Champion at the time who was teaching small groups so that each student could have her own pole. So, again, I reached out. Another first lesson was arranged and nothing was going to stop me from doing this. But torrential rain, no signs for the studio and extreme darkness on a cold winter night almost did. I was, literally, hooked.

Within six months my instructor became more of a mentor and I was encouraged to take the instructor course and a short time after that I was offered the opportunity to take over the studio. I was also encouraged to take fitness seriously as a profession because it came across as being "my natural thing to do". For a few months this became my job after my day job until the latter came to a sudden but not unexpected end.

For months the pole studio was practically my only source of income but it wasn't enough to survive on. I had zero marketing skills AND in the aftermath of becoming unemployed I had forgotten all the amazing things I had achieved so far. It was a gigantic struggle at times just to stay afloat.

I took a year out from working to gain the qualifications I needed to get insurance as a Fitness Professional and work in gyms as a Personal Trainer. During that time I found myself under a lot of stress over all sorts of things that were going wrong in my life and as a consequence I became very ill from chronic fatigue. I decided to give up the pole fitness and concentrate on working with clients who wanted to lose weight and improve their fitness while researching ways of overcoming my own health issues.

It was probably one of the best learning opportunities I had since I became a fitness professional. I now know so much about how the human body works and the many strategies to adopt to ensure it achieves optimum health.

However although my marketing skills were now better, the courage to implement the strategies I learned was close to zero and I was relying on somebody else to do this for me. It worked for a few years but then this system gradually produced less and less results and so I was back to square one.

Things really started to change for the better after I met Hélène again after a year or so at a networking event. We started to meet up regularly and became accountability partners to help each other give our respective businesses direction and move forwards with our many PHDs (Projects Half Done). As one of my marketing coaches pointed out I was great at doing all the work and transforming my clients' lives but, ironically, I never told anyone what my business was called (SMART Fitness Makeover) and so nobody really knew who I was and what I was all about.

Hélène pushed me out of my comfort zone and dragged me to a networking event where I was challenged to... err... take part in a blogging challenge and I jumped in straight away. I think, for the first time ever, I was actually looking forward to telling people all about my work, clients' stories, successes, strategies and so on. After the initial cringing days this became second nature and received excellent feedback for my posts and started to drive traffic to my website.

While in the middle of the blogging challenge Hélène, who had started the same exercise too by then, came up with the idea of making a vlog (video blog) post as a joint effort. Despite all the time I

*spent dancing on stage as a young teenager
nowadays I really hate the thought of being the
centre of too much attention however I am also
aware of the power of videos in marketing so I
went for it and did it.*

*Thanks to Hélène's style of coaching this process
was enjoyable and not at all as painful as I had
imagined it to be. Because by the time I finished
saying something like "OMG my video face is
terrible" Hélène had already plastered her social
media channels with the link to the video it was too
late to back pedal and so I started to do the same
on my own social media channels.*

*I am now no longer scared of the thought of putting
myself out there in this way. In fact, I think it's a
wonderful way to reach out to potential clients who
might not otherwise know that there is somebody
out there who can help them transform their lives
for the better.*

***A lot of Hélène's work is about helping people
become more confident and not being afraid of
expressing themselves. She certainly helped me
massively in this respect, especially with
reconnecting with my inner confidence and sense***

of adventure that I thought I lost forever during a difficult time.

*As it turns out I am glad I allowed her to push me because by **expressing myself and my values,** I am now attracting clients who are a better fit for me and who get what I do and are so happy with the results they are getting they recommend me to their friends and colleagues, thus eliminating the need for me to do any marketing at all!*

Thank you, Cristina for sharing your Extraordinary story with my readers in my book.

CONCLUSION

Once upon a time
There was a story
Your story
That needs to be told
To be heard
To be said
To be articulated

Once upon a time
There was a voice
Your voice
That needs to be heard
To say
Simply, firmly, assertively
With kindness to yourself and to others
With directness and clarity of mind
With happiness and joy

Once upon a time
There was an individual
Who just wanted to say
Articulate, enunciate,
Discuss, debate, speak, talk
With no fear of being judged
No fear of being picked on
No fear of getting it wrong or even right
With assertiveness and joy and happiness

Once upon a time
There is YOU

When are you starting to make yourself heard?
Start now, slowly but surely
Slowly, but setting your own boundaries
In your time and,
When you are ready
From where you are,
On your terms,
Slowly but firmly, proudly

But just
Start.....
I look forward to hearing YOU

Hélène

Remember!

THE 5 KEYS TO UNLOCK YOUR OUTRAGEOUS EXPRESSION

1. *Be Yourself*
2. *Be Kind to Yourself*
3. *Practise*
4. *Have Fun*
5. *Discover your Extraordinary Story*

TESTIMONIALS FOR HÉLÈNE

"Without Hélène's help I would have really struggled to hold it together last night. Thank you Hélène, I will be coming back for more! Yes, thank you Hélène for supporting and guiding us to face standing up and sharing with all the fabulous women. I hope we have set a precedent for other winning women to stand up and share their stories and services".

Jan Cheswright
NLP coach and hypnotherapist

"Thank you Hélène for helping me find the courage to speak last night. Your courses are excellent and definitely worth attending."

Jackie Hopper, *homeopath*

"Really enjoyable course, interactive, Hélène, great trainer, was engaged throughout, could have gone on longer, Highly recommend. Thank you".

Andrea Hall

"Hélène was very clear with her instructions. She is supportive, inspiring and it was fun. I will attend course 2".

Victoria Gerlis

Didn't know what to expect but very glad I went! Really interesting, informative and loads of opportunities to practise what you learn. Warm, friendly and non-judgemental atmosphere.

Hélène has promised a follow-up course (Public Speaking Demystified - part 2) and I will definitely be going!

Brilliant!

Rob Dodwell

"I learned so much from Hélène and it is largely because of her that I am able to run my own events and feel comfortable speaking, which is something I never imagined would happen.

When I first attended one of Hélène 's short courses I was nervous even to stand in front of the group to speak. I had been trained in advocacy for my profession but speaking from the heart was something different! In a couple of hours Hélène showed me how to connect with an audience and gave me the confidence I needed to make a start. Later, I attended a one day course with Hélène which really helped me to build a solid foundation. I learned to deliver my message and to feel confident before an audience. The experience was fun and inspiring and I felt comfortable in the safe space that Hélène held for us. I was also lucky enough to experience a transformational afternoon during which Hélène coached me in speaking in front of a camera. I went from awkward to poised in a few short hours and a whole world of new possibilities opened up for me. I now have the confidence to host my own events, to grasp with both hands any opportunities to speak no matter how large the audience, and I have the wonderful gift of knowing that public speaking can be enjoyable and fulfilling, rather than terrifying. Thanks, Hélène !"

Harriet Balcombe

Mind Calm coach

Stepped out of my comfort zone today, learnt lots and about me, thank you Hélène you amazing lady, Loved loved loved today. Thank you Hélène for today, I attended Public Speaking Demystified level one, I really enjoyed the day great group and a fab trainer, really enjoyed your training techniques and I will/look forward to putting those into practice. Anyone that's a bundle of nerves like me speaking do see Helene

Andrea Hall

Hélène created a safe, nurturing environment where we started the process of communicating and expressing ourselves with vulnerability and with confidence

Julia Meehan-Thompson

Really enjoyable course, interactive, Hélène , great trainer, was engaged throughout, could have gone on longer, Highly recommend. Thank you.

Andrea Hall

I enjoyed the course as it helped me to understand myself and basic of public speaking, it helped me to interact with ease in a group and to express myself. It helped me to understand my strengths and change the perception of myself when it comes to speaking. I would certainly recommend the course to anyone who wishes to speak in public.

Shiva Shankar, *Doctor*

"It was very interactive and energizing course. Helene created positive and friendly atmosphere which helped me to feel safe. I'm glad I joined the workshop and I'll recommend to anyone who would like to improve his confidence.

By the way, you've mention that I'll see the gradual improvement. I think I started to see the results now. I went for some birthday party just after Christmas where

I knew one person and briefly one couple (it was about 30 people in different age). I was quite calm and confident I have to say. Very unusual for me normally I would be stressed and would like to run away ASAP."

Beata Diakowska

....

ABOUT HÉLÈNE MUSSO

Hélène-mother-friend-daughter-inspiring -enthusiastic-passionate-trainer-motivator-facilitator-business owner-dreamer.

Hélène arrived in 1989 in England from France in search of herself with two degrees and an appetite for life. "Nothing ventured, nothing gained" was her motto and with a little experience of drama, she trained and became, in 1993, a Drama teacher and started teaching in Essex.

If you meet her in Essex, she is likely to have taught your son or daughter, your grandchildren and even maybe your great grandchildren. She also worked as an advocate for Creative Partnerships and has been able to shape the teaching and learning in schools through that programme. She is a firm believer in getting learners engaged in their learning with a range of interactive and creative methods.

She still teaches in schools and has a fast and dynamic manner to teaching, making sure you are fully involved and that you can express yourself even if you feel terrified! She aims to create a safe and supportive environment for you to try out and learn from your mistakes.

She is an experienced trainer and facilitator and has previously worked for Creative Partnerships Thames Gateway, Royal Opera House, Protocol teachers, Step Teachers, Keymed, Future Creative, and A New Direction to mention just a few.

She trained in 2014 as an Neuro Linguistic Programming coach and practitioner with John Seymour NLP and has been on a mission to get individuals and businesses expressing themselves!

Most importantly she believes that we have to find OUR own way to express ourselves and that we are the results of a wide range of experiences and there is not one and only recipe to expressing yourself and to happiness. It is by embracing who you are with your imperfections and your vulnerability that you will be able to really find your voice.

She wishes you well on this interesting and at times frustrating journey. Just enjoy every minute of it, even if the ride is bumpy. Value the highs and the lows and develop your confidence on the way.

She runs Public Speaking Demystified, a training company and she helps individuals and businesses to overcome their fears of speaking in public and to make the most amazing presentations with confidence and assurance. You can find her on Hélènemusso.com or email her on beconfident@Hélènemusso.com

RECOMMENDED RESOURCES

If your run your own small business, get into networking. This is the group I have found the most supportive:

Winning Women Essex,

Meetup group in Essex run by Rosemary Cunningham

Winning Women meetups provide a safe, non-judgmental, and inspiring place for heart-centred women in business to come together and learn. This is a place to connect and collaborate with like-minded women on a shared journey, and to get away from the isolation of working alone.

http://www.meetup.com/Winning-Women-Essex/

Our group is based on the following core values.

Connect ~ to bring together entrepreneurial women across the globe (wherever you may be in your journey). We have a sister group that we support in Zambia!

Collaborate ~ to willingly and openly assist each other in making a bigger impact for the greater good of all.

Champion ~ to nurture, support and value every Winning Woman following our philosophy that it's not about ME it's about 'WE'.

Contribute ~ to play a significant role in bringing about learning, to share our talents, gifts and knowledge for personal and professional growth and giving back to the world.

Celebrate ~ to join us in acknowledging the joy and success of others.

Cristina Alciati

Cristina Alciati is the owner of Smart Fitness Makeover, utilising her experience as a lifelong dangerous sports athlete to help women around the world take charge of their health and fitness to live a happier and more fulfilling life while looking fabulous in the process.

A founder member of the Essex Wankelist Massive, she is currently living her Parkour dream in between clients, websites, writing, learning, reading, marketing, networking, consulting and occasionally chilling.

Find her at: SMART Fitness Makeover.com

Wendy Aridela

Wendy Aridela's mission is to help you to make more money from your skills and expertise, so that you can help more people and make a bigger difference in the world.

If you feel you've got a book in you, and you'd love to write it and see it published, get in touch! I offer wrap-around packages that will take you from planning your book to holding it in your hands in just 6 months.

These include regular Skype sessions to keep you on track and personal contact via email plus practical help with editing and formatting your book for publication.

Find me at: wendyaridela.co.uk

John Seymour NLP

My Neuro Linguistic Programming training as a practitioner and coach was based in Bristol and has been life transforming. I highly recommend John Seymour for his training.

http://www.jsnlp.co.uk/

Best Books

Susan Jeffers. Feel the fear and do it anyway.

Louise Hay. The power within.

Stephen R. Covey. The 7 habits of Highly Effective People.

Charles Duhigg. The power of Habit, Why we do what do and how to change?

Romilla Ready and Kate Burton. Neuro Linguistic for Dummies.

Robin Skynner and John Cleese, Life and how to survive it.

Ori and Rom Brafman, Click, The power of Instant Connections.

Guy Claxton. Be Creative, Essential steps to revitalize your work and life.

Edward De Bono. How to have a Beautiful Mind.

ACKNOWLEDGMENTS

I would like to thank thousands of people who have shaped my life and only a few will be mentioned here. I could write pages and pages of names!

I would like to thank **Rosemary Cunningham**, from the Winning Women Essex group, who has been a continuous source of support.

Liz Ware for supporting my ideas online.

Harriet Stack for being a faithful and devoted client and friend.

David Baker for giving me courage.

Wendy Aridela, my book coach for putting up with my scatty thinking.

Cristina Alciati for helping me cope with my own fears of the internet and being a faithful friend.

Pradip Mistry from the Essex Coaching Association for loving my enthusiasm.

Sharon Morse from the Association for Coaching for being so supportive.

Christine Michaelis for her support.

A huge thank you to **Pixabay** especially **Geralt** and **John Hain** who have inspired my book with their beautiful artwork. Pixabay.com is an invaluable resource for free commercial use of pictures.

I would like to thank all my lodgers/guests who have allowed me time to write this book and to mention only one **Maria Carmen Ortola** who was my first lodger and who supported me so much with her kindness!

I would like to thank all the women I have met in the different business groups in England who have contributed to me refining and clarifying my ideas.

I would like to thank **my parents** for giving me the strength to write this book, **my sisters** for looking after me.

I especially want to thank my beautiful children, **Leon Biddle**, my gorgeous son for just loving me unconditionally and my wonderful daughter, **Lily Jordan** for putting up with me on an everyday basis and for challenging my thinking.

Thank you so much for reading my book.

Pass it on to a friend!

Get in touch!

Helenemusso.com

BeConfident@helenemusso.com

Facebook: Public Speaking Demystified: Tame the Fear or Helene Musso

Printed in Great Britain
by Amazon